THE ROCKEFELLERS
AT WILLIAMSBURG

PRECEDING PAGES: THE GOVERNOR'S
PALACE UNDER A BLANKET OF SNOW.

THE POWELL-WALLER GARDEN
(OPPOSITE) TYPIFIES THE BEAUTY
OF WILLIAMSBURG'S GARDENS.

THE DUKE OF GLOUCESTER STREET
(ABOVE) EXTENDS FROM
THE CAPITOL TO THE COLLEGE OF
WILLIAM AND MARY.

THE GUARD HOUSE AND POWDER
MAGAZINE (LEFT) WERE VITAL TO
THE TOWN'S SECURITY.

A YOUNG UNIFORMED GROOMSMAN (ABOVE) CUTS A FINE FIGURE RIDING BRISKLY
IN A COLONIAL CARRIAGE.

CRAFTSMEN IN COLONIAL ATTIRE UNLOAD AN OX CART AT THE NORTON COLE HOUSE
IN WILLIAMSBURG'S HISTORIC AREA.

THE ROCKEFELLERS AT WILLIAMSBURG

Backstage with the Founders, Restorers and World-Renowned Guests

CHRONICLED BY DONALD J. GONZALES

EPM

EPM PUBLICATIONS, INC., McLEAN, VIRGINIA

Library of Congress Cataloging-in-Publication Data

Gonzales, Donald J.
    The Rockefellers at Williamsburg: Backstage with the founders, restorers and world-renowned guests / Donald J. Gonzales.
        p.   cm.
    Includes index
    ISBN 0−939009−58−7 — ISBN 0−939009−53−6 (pbk.)
    1. Williamsburg (Va.) — History. 2. Celebrities — Virginia — Williamsburg — History — 20th century. 3. Rockefeller, Winthrop, 1912−1973. 4. Rockefeller, John D. (John Davison), 1874−1960.
    I. Title
    F234.W7G46 199   191−18708
    975.5′4252—dc20

EPM Publications, Inc., 1003 Turkey Run Road, McLean, Virginia 22101

Printed in the United States of America

THE ROCKEFELLERS AT WILLIAMSBURG is published simultaneously in hard and soft cover.

The author gratefully acknowledges the use of photographs from The Colonial Williamsburg Foundation. Six of them (on pages 41, 42, 45, 46 and 47) were published in *Bassett Hall: The Williamsburg Home of Mr. and Mrs. John D. Rockefeller, Jr.,* © 1984 by The Colonial Williamsburg Foundation. Any sources other than The Foundation are credited individually.

Cover: The Duke of Gloucester Street, Colonial Williamsburg.

Frontispiece: John D. Rockefeller, Jr., and the Reverend W. A. R. Goodwin envisioned a lasting, inspiring future for Colonial Williamsburg.

Book design by Robert Wiser/Archetype Press, Washington, D.C.

Dedicated

to

Mary Tolhurst Gonzales,

our family

and

readers of the present,

and more especially those of the future,

who may have an interest

in the establishment of Colonial Williamsburg

and its development and expansion

into a world-renowned cultural institution

CONTENTS

PROLOGUE
16

WINTHROP ROCKEFELLER, CATTLEMAN
18

JOHN D. ROCKEFELLER, JR., PATRIOT
25

THE ROCKEFELLERS SETTLE IN
33

BASSETT HALL, A COLONIAL HAVEN
40

FROM FATHER TO SON TO SON
51

PROVIDING THE FINANCIAL BACKBONE
63

ROCKEFELLERS TO READER'S DIGEST TO THE FUTURE
68

PRESIDENT JOHNSON FOLLOWS THOMAS JEFFERSON
77

EISENHOWER AND CHURCHILL
84

JAMES MICHENER, "FRIEND AND WRITER"
93

ROMANCING NORMAN ROCKWELL
96

VIP PARADE
102

WILLIAMSBURG AND RICHMOND
124

LIGHTER MOMENTS BEHIND THE SCENES
131

A RACE WITH RACE RELATIONS
138

PRESIDENTIAL "SEARCH" BEGINS
144

EPILOGUE
150

Heads of State and Dignitaries Who Have Visited Colonial Williamsburg, 1953–1990
151

Index
157

About the Author
160

MR. AND MRS. JOHN D.
ROCKEFELLER, JR. (OPPOSITE),
AFTER ATTENDING A
CEREMONY HELD AT THE
MATTHEW WHALEY
ELEMENTARY SCHOOL IN
WILLIAMSBURG.

CHURCHILL AND EISENHOWER
TAKING THE OFFICIAL TOUR
BY COLONIAL CARRIAGE WITH
JOHN D. ROCKEFELLER 3RD,
CHAIRMAN OF THE BOARD.

SONS LAURANCE,
WINTHROP AND NELSON
(LEFT) ATTENDING THE
OPENING OF THE
ABBY ALDRICH ROCKEFELLER
FOLK ART CENTER.

PROLOGUE

The idea for this book came from Winthrop Rockefeller in the 1960s when he was serving as Governor of Arkansas and Chairman of the Board of Trustees of The Colonial Williamsburg Foundation. It was soon after noon when the telephone rang at our home, the Robert Carter House, located adjacent to the Governor's Palace in Williamsburg. It was Winthrop. He had some time on his hands midday on a Sunday after a trustees' meeting, he said. His airplane would be two hours late leaving Arkansas, and he asked my wife, Mary, and me if we were available "to talk a while." We were.

Winthrop was in a mellow mood as we sat in the living room of Colonial Williamsburg's VIP residential headquarters, the Lightfoot House. "Win" had been thinking, he said, about my previous United Press writing background at the White House, State Department and United Nations. He thought I might find some interesting material for a book some day on the Rockefeller family and their relationship, particularly that of his father, with the restoration of Williamsburg. He suggested that to do this I should begin at the Rockefeller Archive Center in Pocantico Hills, the family estate in New York, and meet Joseph W. Ernst, the director. It was impossible then to break away from my duties at Williamsburg to pursue his proposal, but about twenty years later, I met Ernst for luncheon at the Williamsburg Inn. And several years after that meeting I finally visited the Archive on the first of several visits.

My only solace in taking so long traces to what James Michener, a frequent Williamsburg visitor, once told me. He said he did not write a book about a region until he had visited it many times. In this case I write about Williamsburg only after having lived in its Historic Area for thirty years!

During the many years since that conversation with Winthrop Rockefeller, I accumulated a wealth of experience watching the colonial village become an international crossroads. I also gained first-hand experience with the Rockefeller family, working for three decades with various members and their top aides in a number of preservation, conservation and education projects in many states.

After spending twenty-five years inside Colonial Williamsburg, I retired as Senior Vice President and took up consulting work with the restoration organization and other Rockefeller projects. Assignments led me to Rockefeller destinations in New York City, including International House, long a haven for thousands of Americans and students from abroad; to Bradford College in Massachusetts; to Winthrop Rockefeller's sprawling cattle farm at Petit Jean

Mountain near Morrilton, Arkansas; and to Laurance and Mary Rockefeller's extensive interests in Woodstock, Vermont. Another fascinating area where I spent a great deal of time was New York's Hudson River Valley. There the Rockefellers have been associated for generations with Sleepy Hollow Restorations (now Historic Hudson Valley): Washington Irving's home and Philipsburg Manor in Tarrytown; Van Cortlandt Manor at Croton-on-Hudson; and, later on, north up the Hudson River to Montgomery Place at Annandale-on-Hudson. Along the way I was privileged to visit on several occasions the Rockefeller family estate at Pocantico, New York; the Rockefeller home at Woodstock, Vermont; Bassett Hall (their Williamsburg home); and the Governor's Mansion and office in Little Rock when Winthrop Rockefeller was Governor there.

From my experience in these locations, at other Rockefeller places and my Williamsburg background, it occurred to me I could trace the Williamsburg story and link it to the Rockefellers in a new way. As part of my research in New York, I found extensive information on Williamsburg in the 1930s that was unavailable in the colonial city. This data provided new insights into the early days of the restoration, particularly from the point of view and experiences of Rockefeller associates, who saw the project from a metropolitan distance and as part of many other world-wide philanthropic interests.

Another advantage of writing the book now rather than earlier is the benefit of research done by others during the past thirty-plus years. For example, in 1988, *The Rockefeller Century* by John Ensor Harr and Peter J. Johnson added new depth to the Williamsburg story, and more will come in a second volume. Also, Carlisle H. Humelsine, President and Chairman of the Board of Colonial Williamsburg, and I collaborated over the years on many publications, including annual reports, speeches, articles in *Colonial Williamsburg Today*, etc. One pamphlet, entitled *Reflections of John D. Rockefeller, Jr., in Williamsburg, 1926–1960*, issued on the twenty-fifth anniversary of Mr. Rockefeller's death, summed up Humelsine's long association with the benefactor of Williamsburg. It has provided a valuable record for this longer publication.

During the years, many old records have finally come to light. Oral histories, including nearly 300 pages of my own recollections, have been assembled by Colonial Williamsburg. Other new productive research has been completed. The Williamsburg story grows and is certain to expand into even richer detail in the future.

The pages that follow are in part a personal memoir, an effort to gather the high points of an odyssey that no one could have forecast, a career that never went according to any grand plan, fortunately. They are also a saga of a kid from the village of Elmwood, Nebraska (population 414), who, with his Elmwood sweetheart and through his long association with the Rockefellers, has dined at the White House, the State Department and Colonial Williamsburg with kings, queens, prime ministers, dignitaries and VIPs from around the world.

I hope the following fulfills what Winthrop Rockefeller had in mind so long ago.

DONALD J. GONZALES
INTERLOCHEN, MICHIGAN
MANZANILLO-SANTIAGO, MEXICO
AND WILLIAMSBURG, VIRGINIA

WINTHROP ROCKEFELLER, CATTLEMAN

Much to my surprise, my life began changing course one morning in March 1958. The telephone rang at my booth in the State Department news room, where I worked as the diplomatic correspondent for the United Press (no UPI at that time). It was a long-time friend, Carlisle H. Humelsine, advising me he would be elected President of Colonial Williamsburg in May 1958. I told him I didn't have time to hear about his new life in Colonial Williamsburg or his quick suggestion that I might consider joining him.

"You know Dulles holds a news conference every Tuesday at 11," I said hastily. "It's 11 now. If you don't get off the phone, I'll need another job."

However, I promised to call him back. Not believing he was serious about the job offer, I let days go by. Finally, several weeks later we got together in Williamsburg.

Humelsine was persuasive. He mentioned that United Press had no retirement program; Colonial Williamsburg did—and it might be sweetened. That got my attention. He pointed out I would be given a home at reasonable rent. Further, he hit at the time I had posted a notice on the entrance to my press room booth. It stated, "Most people who are going to change jobs change by age 40." I was thirty-nine-plus.

Finally, I saw real merit—and more money—and accepted Humelsine's various blandishments to become Vice President of Colonial Williamsburg for Public Relations.

Humelsine then said the next hurdle was for me to meet Winthrop Rockefeller, Chairman of the Board of Colonial Williamsburg and Arkansas cattle rancher. He hinted the meeting probably would be pro forma and definitely interesting, no matter the outcome. It certainly was that! For one thing, the get-together turned out to be one of those times when nothing goes right. The interview almost didn't happen. Overall, there were enough hitches to remind me several times that I was still fully employed at United Press; I hadn't sought this job in the first place! But throughout the ordeal I found Winthrop delightful and undaunted by the series of setbacks we initially encountered. In fact, this meeting, when we finally did get together, set the stage for a stronger future relationship.

WINTHROP ROCKEFELLER ON HIS CATTLE FARM AT WINROCK, ARKANSAS.
(ROCKEFELLER ARCHIVE CENTER, PHOTO BY WILLIAM E. DAVIS)

Humelsine made the arrangements for Rockefeller and me to meet on my day off. He wrote me saying:

> As I told you, Mr. Rockefeller will be flying to New York from the farm in Arkansas on Monday. He is planning to break the trip at Washington, and will meet you around 2:30 at the Butler Aviation Terminal. I imagine that he will take you over to the American Airlines' Admirals Club and will probably have an hour or so to chat with you. The purpose of this meeting is for you two to take a look at one another and get acquainted. I suggest that you do not talk to him about arrangements, as he will not be involved in any of the administrative matters in connection with filling this position. Just be your natural self with Mr. Rockefeller. He is a very easy-going and relaxed individual and I believe that you will enjoy him.

At 3:00 P.M. I was paged, "Mr. Rockefeller wants you to know he is late leaving Arkansas. He would understand completely if you can't wait." I was pleased a Rockefeller would contact me at all. This was my first experience with a new time zone, one I soon had to accommodate. The nation, of course, has several established time zones, but I learned another one—"Winrock Time." Rockefeller had a consistent tendency to run late. And so what, as long as you have your own plane—a form of independence I came to covet.

Winthrop Rockefeller finally arrived in Washington at 5:00 P.M. He was in no hurry to cut the interview short and make up time to New York. As he straightened up after squeezing through the oval door of his plane, he looked enormous, even formidable. I judged him to be around 6′4″, 250 pounds. Then I saw his handlebar moustache and a twenty-gallon (at least) ranch hat. After a strong handshake he excused himself to climb back into the plane. He reappeared with a bottle of Dewar's Scotch wrapped in a newspaper!

By auto we were whisked up the flight ramp to the Admirals Club. After he pushed the buzzer we stepped up to a reception desk. The "sentry" was a stocky fellow who knew his responsibilities.

"Are you a member here?" he asked Rockefeller.

"No, but my brother is," Win replied.

"Who's your brother?"

"Laurance Rockefeller."

"Won't do you any good here."

"I'm a member in Dallas."

"Nope."

Then Win told him about the arrangements Humelsine had made for a brief sit-down meeting. I stepped back, looked to the ceiling, put my hands up in a silent appeal for the receptionist to please relent. That seemed to help.

"Well, okay," the young man said. "If you won't tell anybody."

Winthrop pledged eternal secrecy!

Our meeting lasted until 7:00 P.M. It covered everything except Williamsburg—and with lots of Scotch. We talked about Win's interest in cattle and airplanes (after he found out I had been a World War II pilot). He talked about his father, his mother and brothers, how the brothers didn't cross over into each other's spheres of interest, but how they met once or twice a year in New York to discuss their individual and mutual interests. I was fascinated by his World War II career in the army, how he was wounded at Iwo Jima.

"How did you get into the army?" I asked.

"Oh," he replied, "my brothers and I were meeting in New York before the war. It seemed certain the United States would enter the conflict, and because of our stake in America we decided one of us (Laurance, John 3rd, Nelson, David, Winthrop) should volunteer. We all looked around the table. It suddenly occurred to me I was the only one who was single. So I volunteered to enlist in the army."

With this insight into family operations the conversation turned briefly to Williamsburg. Winthrop alluded to his father's deep interest in the project and then mentioned that his brother, John 3rd, and his father had not seen eye-to-eye on the future of the restoration project. This disagreement, Winthrop pointed out, was the reason he was Chairman of the Board of Colonial Williamsburg, succeeding John 3rd. I didn't know what he was really touching on, but left it alone.

On this indefinite note the meeting began winding down. We returned to the desk. It was quickly clear why our reception there had been awkward, to say the least. A very attractive hostess was on duty in place of the somewhat pugnacious young man who had first attended us. She apparently had been on a break when we first arrived. Upon returning she had heard from the young man (who turned out to be the bartender) how he had reluctantly let that Rockefeller fellow into the hallowed halls of The Club! The hostess valiantly tried to make amends, to pick up the pieces.

"Oh, Mr. Rockefeller," she said brightly, eyeing his big Western hat, "I see you are a cowboy!"

"Cattleman, Ma'am," Winthrop said in a quick way that disclosed his dislike for any cowboy analogies.

She tried again, looking down at his alligator boots. His "WR" initials were impressed upon the sides.

"What lovely cowboy boots you have," she chirped.

"Cattleman's boots," Winthrop replied, with a clear and final inflection that ended the hopeless exchange. I, too, was looking for an escape.

Then Winthrop turned to me and began a motion I learned was a fairly regular gesture of his. He patted his trousers' pockets, fore and aft, not once but several times, then he searched his shirt pockets and jacket. I realized, just as he admitted, he had no money!

"Don," he asked, "do you have any money? I want to tip that nice young man who let us in."

I coughed up my last five dollars—loaned it to a Rockefeller! Well, it turned out I really donated the five bucks to him. It was an experience I was to encounter frequently as we met more often.

At any rate, some four hours behind schedule (and five dollars lighter) I waved goodbye to Winthrop Rockefeller, not knowing what to make of the afternoon's on-again-off-again events. When I reported on the meeting to Humelsine, he told me the interview had gone well as far as Winthrop was concerned. I couldn't have been more surprised. I had the Williamsburg job, if I wanted it.

More than a month later, after I had moved to Williamsburg, I met Winthrop again, this time in the East Lounge of the Williamsburg Inn.

"Mr. Rockefeller," I said. "It's good to see you again."

"Just call me Win," he replied.

There was no mention of the five bucks.

I encountered one more hurdle neither Humelsine nor I had anticipated, one unrelated to whether I got the job; I was already there and signed in. The unexpected incident was the cool welcome I received from Kenneth Chorley, the outgoing President of Colonial Williamsburg. Unaware of a sensitive situation, Humelsine said on my first day he would like to introduce me to Chorley, and by appointment we walked into the President's office.

Chorley did not get up from his chair. He did not offer me his hand. I wondered how much this meeting was going to cost me, possibly $10?

Carl, sensing all was not well, gave it his best try.

"Kenneth, you'll recall that Earl Newsome and Company once tried to hire Don to be the Washington representative of Reynolds Metals Company."

Silence.

"And," continued Carl, "that Don was a Nieman Fellow at Harvard." Chorley didn't bat an eye, nor utter a word.

After several other sterling efforts, there was nothing more to say; Chorley leaned back, looked out the window, checked the ceiling and finally said:

"Do you know you are the first administrative officer hired here in more than twenty years that I have not approved; I've hired every other one that's here, including Carl."

That was the first time I realized how special my appointment was.

Chorley also hinted that to work in Williamsburg you needed more than sixteen years of experience dealing with United States presidents, secretaries of state, foreign ministers and the like; more than I had from being a test pilot in the Army Air Corps. I recognized that morning there were some *real gaps* in my background.

What, I wondered, am I doing here? The tension eased. We were asked to sit down. Though I couldn't have imagined it that day, it did come to pass that over a period of years I did gain Chorley's wary acknowledgment, if not approval.

It was a good thing my day-to-day bosses were Rockefeller and Humelsine, and as time passed I came to admire their extraordinary insights and judgments in quickly handling problems that would have required committee deliberations by other executives. With this in mind, any recollection of Winthrop Rockefeller in the early days of our relationship has to include an exchange we had far into the night when I was at the ranch in Arkansas to assist on several projects. I received a call from Winthrop at 11:00 P.M. in my bedroom. He was at the main house several hundred yards up the mountain.

"Are you still up, Don?" Winthrop asked.

"Oh sure," I replied (although I was in pajamas).

"I've just gotten home from Little Rock. I'll come down."

"No need, I'll come up."

We talked until 4:00 A.M. about Rockefeller's decision to declare two days hence as a Republican candidate for Governor of Arkansas. Many obstacles were discussed that night: how

he would be reviled by Governor Orville Faubus; how he could expect political trouble from his ex-wife, Bobo, and public screening of other aspects of his personal life; how he would have to diminish his cattle interests and lead a much more public political life. As the hours moved on to daylight we walked to the rim of Petit Jean Mountain overlooking the Arkansas River below. We stopped at the edge of a garden, and he pointed to a brass plaque that carried his mother's favorite quote from Micah 6:8, " . . . and what doth the Lord require of thee, but to do justly and to love mercy, and to walk humbly with thy God?"

I was struck by the emotional impact this verse had on Winthrop, who, for much of his life, had quite a different reputation—one not considered "Biblical."

Then I asked Winthrop what he figured his chances were of becoming Governor. I was questioning why he should expose himself to all the problems looming ahead.

"Oh," he replied matter-of-factly, "I'll lose the first time I try. But I'll win the next time around."

"Win, I really don't know why you're going ahead with this," I observed.

The answer came quickly, "Because I ought to!" This startled me. Then I understood. This was the Rockefeller credo of his and his parents' generation—commitment that required them to give up so much of their privacy. It was their innate sense of responsible destiny that kept them from frittering away and wasting their wealth and time. It was the force that made them seek and succeed at projects for the public good—and behind all of it was the "humble" quote from Micah.

While in Williamsburg some years later, Winthrop, after being elected Governor, learned by telephone that a bloody prison riot was under way in Arkansas. When he came back to the room in the Abby Aldrich Rockefeller Folk Art Center, Winthrop signaled to me to sit with him on a bench. He told me about the prison crisis, then looked at the floor, silent. When he looked up, he asked, "What was that you said I told you that night we talked at the farm?" When I grasped what he meant I replied, "You told me you were going to run for Governor of Arkansas because you ought to." He shook his head, got up slowly, and we rejoined the party.

JOHN D. ROCKEFELLER, JR., PATRIOT

I n May 1958, Carlisle H. Humelsine was elected President of Colonial Williamsburg, succeeding Kenneth Chorley, an English-born giant of a gentleman who held
the top job at Williamsburg for twenty-three years. Concurrently, Chorley also
served as John D. Rockefeller, Jr.'s aide in New York and spent most of his time there
rather than in Williamsburg.

On May 21, 1958, the day the presidential transition took place, I was asked
to go with Chorley and Humelsine to Bassett Hall (the Rockefellers' Williamsburg home
adjacent to the Historic Area) to meet John D. Rockefeller, Jr. While posing for photographs,
Rockefeller spoke of his long affection for Williamsburg and how much more he felt at home
in the old village than in New York. He expressed his faith in Humelsine and the future of
the restoration organization. The three laughed as Chorley and Rockefeller delved deeply
into the early days of the restoration of Williamsburg and their experiences. Rockefeller was
most cordial while shaking hands. He knew who I was and what my starting job was to be.
I was struck by Rockefeller's pleasant urbanity and spontaneous wit. From afar I had always
heard how kind of stiff he was unless he was meeting people. I came away that day thinking
of Rockefeller as a warm grandfatherly type. I was ready to join his team.

Thus began my immersion into the established history of Williamsburg and its emerg-
ing role as an important guide to the present and future.

John D. Rockefeller, Jr., the heir to his father's immense fortune, had learned early to be
on the lookout for opportunists who tried to invade his pockets for their own gain. Though
at first he fended off the determined Episcopal minister bent on finding a million or so, he
ultimately realized he had met his match.

The Reverend W. A. R. Goodwin clearly felt he had God's support in his quest for a benefactor who could save and restore the little village of Williamsburg. It nevertheless took all
of his considerable skills to see his passionate vision fulfilled: the restoration of the eighteenth-century capital of the Virginia colony. The reverend's dual role as rector of Bruton
Parish Church and professor of Biblical literature and religious education at The College of
William and Mary in Virginia enabled him to see past Williamsburg's dusty streets of the

JOHN D. ROCKEFELLER, JR., WITH THE REVEREND W.A.R. GOODWIN IN BRUTON PARISH
CHURCHYARD, TURNING VISION INTO REALITY.

1920s, dilapidated old buildings, broken-down fences and sagging economy to the potential revival of its glorious past. He saw Williamsburg as the original training and testing ground for the birth of a new nation; the place where George Washington, Patrick Henry, Thomas Jefferson, George Mason and other early American patriots had pursued their dreams of democracy. The decrepit state of Williamsburg, however, was hardly one to attract any investors, let alone a Rockefeller.

Never doubting that his cause was just and his dream possible, Goodwin used his persuasive powers on the cautious, conservative and ever-suspicious Rockefeller. The path Goodwin forged is a story of determination without parallel. At times the man of the cloth gave up—almost. But somehow the two men were destined to work together on saving and restoring the hidden but priceless gem of a town. In those birthing days neither man in his wildest dreams suspected that Colonial Williamsburg sixty years later would attract two million visitors annually (only one million buy tickets; the remainder walk in the Historic Area without entering the exhibition buildings) and play host to more than 100 heads of state from all over the world, and that Mr. Rockefeller alone would contribute $70 million to the project—and love it!

The Rockefeller-Goodwin story can be told more fully now than when it began unfolding back in 1926.

At the beginning, Rockefeller didn't realize the power of Goodwin's persuasion, nor the depth of his interest. For one thing, Goodwin had a broad knowledge of history as well as religion. As a boy on a farm in western Virginia, he had saved his money from working in corn fields to buy a book entitled *Buried Cities Recovered*. He kept this treasured book all his life. As the years passed, the young minister was persuaded to leave a parish in Rochester, New York, for Williamsburg—a decision based in large part on an earlier assignment in the old capital. At the time, he wrote with his deep feeling for the Williamsburg of two centuries earlier:

> Intangible, but real; invisible, but ever present, the spirit of the days of long ago haunts and hallows the ancient city and the home of its honored dead; a spirit that stirs the memory and fires the imagination . . . .

Was it any wonder that Rockefeller, exposed to such a man, would wilt in the face of his "fires," his zeal? Guarded and totally unsuspecting of what the village minister had in store for him, the New York philanthropist was already quietly funding huge restoration projects at the Agora, the ancient marketplace in Athens, and the chateau at Versailles outside Paris. The chateau at Fountainbleu and the war-damaged cathedral in Rheims had also drawn his support. In addition, there was Rockefeller funding for extensive archaeological excavations in Egypt and Palestine.

In this country Rockefeller was pouring millions more into conservation efforts in the Shenandoah Mountains, Yellowstone, the Great Smokies, the Palisades and the Hudson River Valley, the Grand Canyon, the Grand Tetons, Yosemite and the California Redwoods. Why would he take on a preservation project in a little corner of Virginia? Some time later, Fairfield Osborn, one of America's foremost conservationists, would supply insight into Rockefeller's motives. He wrote that Rockefeller's depth of feeling and awe for the wonders of nature provided "the vital urge for the preservation of regions of outstanding beauty which he realized,

BRUTON PARISH CHURCH HAS SERVED MANY CONGREGATIONS SINCE
THE FIRST BUILDING WAS ERECTED IN 1683. THIS STRUCTURE WAS BEGUN IN 1712.

if once marred or destroyed, could never be replaced. Concurrently, the preservation of historical monuments became part of the whole broad plan culminating in what is perhaps the most notable task of restoration ever undertaken—that of Colonial Williamsburg."

In Virginia there was also the Episcopal minister, watching, working and waiting for his big moment. Against different and diverse backgrounds, Goodwin and Rockefeller first met at a Phi Beta Kappa banquet in New York City on February 26, 1924. The clergyman had selected Rockefeller as the prime target of his campaign to stop Williamsburg's slide into oblivion. As part of the strategy, Goodwin invited Rockefeller to come to Williamsburg to see his plan to restore the three original buildings at The College of William and Mary: the Brafferton, once used as a school for Indians; the President's House; and the adjacent Wren Building. He pointed out that Presidents Jefferson, Monroe and Tyler were William and Mary alumni. Rockefeller came, was polite, put his hand on his billfold and voiced no particular interest, pointing out it was long-standing family policy to make gifts to educational institutions through the General Education Board.

Feeling the rebuff, Goodwin regrouped and targeted the Ford family in Detroit. He wrote on June 13, 1924, to Edsel Ford:

> Seriously, I want your father to buy Williamsburg, the old Colonial capital of Virginia at a time when Virginia included the land (in Michigan) on which the Ford factory is now located, as in those days the western boundary of Virginia was the Pacific Ocean. . . . Unfortunately, you and your father are at present the chief contributors to the destruction of the city. With the new concrete roads leading from Newport News to Richmond . . . and Jamestown . . . garages and gas tanks are fast spoiling the whole appearance of the old city, and most of the cars which stop at the garages and gas tanks are Ford cars.

The Fords were unimpressed, if not irritated, by the request. They just built more Model T's.

Two years after Goodwin and Rockefeller had first met in New York City, Mr. and Mrs. John D. Rockefeller, Jr., and their sons Laurance, Winthrop and David stopped off briefly in Williamsburg. Goodwin played his hand astutely. Except for guiding a tour of Williamsburg, Jamestown and Yorktown, Goodwin didn't make a move although he felt it "exceedingly hard . . . not to burst forth with the broader, evolving idea of restoring the entire core area of the old capital of the Virginia Colony." Instinct told him that although his concept was expanding, the timing was wrong for a forceful appeal.

Many years later I heard Winthrop reveal some tense and exciting moments of an early family trip to Williamsburg. He told a Colonial Williamsburg Trustee dinner in 1971:

> I was at a rather tender age and that year I had been allowed to drive a very fine Nash. My brother, John, who never did learn to drive very well, was driving Mother and Father in a Lincoln. I was driving the Nash carrying the baggage with Valentine, our chauffeur, who "teached" me how to drive.
>
> My father was a very meticulous man. His attitude was that if you started out on a day's drive and still could squeeze in two gallons more, you put those two gallons in. I didn't do that. We drove and drove and I watched that gas gauge go down, down, down. We got to the Colonial Inn in Williamsburg. After we unloaded the baggage I said to myself, "I must get some gasoline." I drove one block and ran out; but I coasted into a Sinclair station. Being a very faithful

member of the Rockefeller family and Standard-Esso, I refused to buy more than one gallon from Sinclair. With that purchase I went across the street and filled up at a good Esso station.

Thus, Winthrop was introduced to Williamsburg.

The crucial Goodwin-Rockefeller meeting occurred on November 27, 1927, when Rockefeller returned for the dedication of Phi Beta Kappa Memorial Hall at The College of William and Mary. Rockefeller was Phi Beta Kappa from his days at Brown University. This time Goodwin borrowed a limousine and chauffeur. The two men drove around the little town and then took a long walk. That evening Rockefeller finally succumbed—but only for $2,500 to complete a set of drawings and sketches. By the time Rockefeller died in 1960—thirty-four years later—he had committed a whopping $70 million to the restoration and endowment of Colonial Williamsburg!

The best summary of what Rockefeller hoped to accomplish in Williamsburg is outlined in excerpts of a letter dated November 30, 1927, to his aide Colonel Arthur Woods, who became the first President of Colonial Williamsburg:

It is my desire and purpose to carry out this enterprise completely and entirely. Such accomplishment involves in general terms the acquiring of substantially all of the property on the Duke of Gloucester Street from the House of Burgesses to the College grounds, the acquiring of much other property referred to more specifically in the memorandum, the rebuilding of the House of Burgesses and the Palace, the building of the Sir Christopher Wren building on the College campus. The purpose of this undertaking is to restore Williamsburg, so far as that may be possible, to what it was in the old colonial days and to make it a great center for historical study and inspiration.

The project, after it has been completed from a physical point of view, will need an endowment of a million dollars or more, in order to maintain the buildings and insure their being permanently used for the purposes intended. Dr. Goodwin has very wisely suggested that the two blocks on either side of the Duke of Gloucester Street at the College end, which will be most costly to acquire, be used for the construction of appropriate buildings that will adequately house the business needs of the town.

The purpose of this letter is to authorize my office to finance this entire program, whether it costs three or four, or even five millions of dollars, the matter going forward and the specific authorizations being made from time to time generally as set forth in this letter.

Very truly,
/s/ John D. Rockefeller, Jr.

The history of the restoration is filled with local anecdotes about the impact of the New York philanthropist and his kindred spirit, Goodwin. But one account of a real estate transaction tells the story better than any other.

A merchant in "downtown" Williamsburg had a store of the smallest size that had to be purchased for the project. It could not have cost more than a couple of hundred dollars to build, if that. One day, Goodwin asked the merchant how much he wanted for it.

"I want $35,000," was the quick reply.

"Jim, your property isn't worth anything like $35,000," Goodwin said quickly.

"Boss, could you give me $5,000?"

Goodwin said that was fine, but "Why did you start at $35,000 and then in the next breath ask only $5,000?"

"Well, Boss, they told me to start high and come down."

While Rockefeller was always dedicated to the Williamsburg project Goodwin's sense of urgency conflicted sometimes with the New Yorker's somewhat slower sense of timing. Their resulting differences occasionally brought about a testiness in Rockefeller, if not irritability.

One time Rockefeller received an urgent telegram while he was on vacation at Seal Harbor, Maine. The message from a top aide in New York said he had several letters from Dr. Goodwin "urging many purchases not heretofore authorized and not covered by your instructions. Asks for immediate decision on same."

Rockefeller replied the same day from his retreat, "Not disposed to allow Doctor Goodwin to push me into purchases beyond present authorization prior to my return. . . . Am anxious to continue as carefree as possible while here."

Apropos of Rockefeller's reaction is a story told me by Stanley Abbott, superintendent of the Colonial National Historical Park. The Rockefellers had asked him to join them on a trip to Jamestown Island for a picnic.

"We rounded a curve on the island and Rockefeller saw a dead tree with an osprey nest standing alone in the marsh," Abbott said.

"'Abbott, why don't you cut that dead tree down?' Rockefeller asked.

"I told him about the osprey nest and added that I kind of liked the tree for its aesthetic quality. When Mrs. Rockefeller sided with me, Rockefeller told her, 'Well, if you like it so much, maybe I could have it cut down and planted outside your bedroom window at Pocantico' (the Rockefellers' home in New York near Tarrytown). That ended the back-and-forth, and we drove on to the picnic spot."

In time, Rockefeller became more and more enamored of Goodwin's vision and dedication. Goodwin once wrote that he saw the colonial capital as a place where "we can impress upon coming generations deathless ideals. . . . A living shrine that presents a picture, right before our eyes, of the shining days when the great idea was in the crucible of freedom."

The excitement Rockefeller felt was described in Raymond B. Fosdick's *John D. Rockefeller, Jr.—A Portrait*: "Of all the things he ever undertook, Williamsburg seemed to reward him with the greatest satisfaction."

Fosdick observed that "Colonial Williamsburg is undoubtedly the most ambitious restoration project ever undertaken in America. Born of the vaulting imagination of one man and the creative generosity of another, it stands today as a vast and accurate shrine to the nation's past."

After I had been in Williamsburg several years, I had a rare opportunity to learn more, a deeper insight, from Winthrop Rockefeller about his father's and other family members' affection for Williamsburg. During a conversation in the living room of the Moody House on Francis Street, Winthrop drew an analogy between the early American patriots and his father in Williamsburg, a span of 200 years. I wrote this memorandum after the meeting was over:

WINTHROP ROCKEFELLER, THIRD CHAIRMAN OF CW, POSED WITH HIS NIECE, ABBY O'NEILL, LONG AN ACTIVE WILLIAMSBURG TRUSTEE, NOW VICE CHAIRMAN.

Winthrop Rockefeller's "philosophy" and his father's were summed up this general way—"The concept of Colonial Williamsburg is so much bigger than any mortal being . . . father's influence is going to live and influence people for many years to come . . . there is a natural parallel between the courage of this man and the courage of men of the eighteenth century . . . I think of all the men who are living today. . . . I think of Winston Churchill and there are just very few others who can measure up to the eighteenth-century qualities of courage and vision. But father does." Winthrop then referred again to Williamsburg and the need for planning "in perpetuity."

This final statement was of tremendous significance. Often the Rockefellers fund some projects for a limited number of years, say five or so. But the depth of interest and support for Williamsburg has extended for nearly seventy years. Further, the family interest continues strong through Abby and George O'Neill, active members of the Colonial Williamsburg Board of Trustees. Named for her grandmother, Abby Aldrich Rockefeller (Mrs. John D. Rockefeller, Jr.), Abby O'Neill, representing third-generation family presence and support, once referred to Colonial Williamsburg as "my passion."

She has served nearly twenty-five years as a Williamsburg Trustee, including a current assignment as Vice Chairman. Her major interest has been in the authenticity and integrity of the Historic Area and related properties. George O'Neill has served in many Board posts related to hotel operations, auditing, compensation and finance.

Thus, the restoration work started in Williamsburg by the kindred spirits of Rockefeller and Goodwin continues to this day. This unprecedented Rockefeller family interest, now matched by the support of the American people, should assure Williamsburg "in perpetuity."

THE ROCKEFELLERS SETTLE IN

Until mid-year 1928, Rockefeller's name and his involvement in Williamsburg were cloaked in secrecy by Goodwin. The code name, in all Williamsburg-bound correspondence, telegrams and inter-office communication was "David's Father," drawn from Rockefeller's son, David. As events mounted, the populace knew the good rector didn't have money of his own to buy the property he was accumulating. Speculation on the identity of his backer ranged from the Ford family in Michigan to George Eastman in Rochester, New York, where Goodwin had ministered at St. Paul's Church. On June 12, 1928, the secret came out. Goodwin called a town meeting and announced that John D. Rockefeller, Jr., had been visiting Williamsburg secretly, strolling about the old town, and with Goodwin had walked to the Great Oak Tree at Bassett Hall—all the while talking about restoring Williamsburg. The audience was surprised and startled at the disclosure. Many wondered, with some suspicion, why a Rockefeller would want to do such a thing "in an old town like this."

Rockefeller later told a Williamsburg audience that he, too, was surprised at his involvement, quipping, "I'd heard of people being taken for a ride. Dr. Goodwin took me for a walk!"

During their first walk to Bassett Hall and the Great Oak nearly two years before, Rockefeller had admired the huge tree and asked Goodwin:

"If I come back some day, can we bring our lunch down, and eat it under the oak tree?"

Local suspicion of the millionaire's motives gradually faded as John and Abby Rockefeller quietly moved about Williamsburg and became acquainted as "neighbors" with the people of the sleepy little town. One local citizen observed, "One of the nicest things about Mr. and Mrs. Rockefeller was when you were talking with them you had to pinch yourself to believe they were Mr. and Mrs. Rockefeller." Another local said, "My first remembrance of the Rockefellers was seeing Mrs. Rockefeller sitting on a bench in the Courtyard of the Palace. I went to her and asked if she wouldn't come in. She said she couldn't because she didn't have any money—she was waiting for John to bring her fifty cents to buy a ticket. When he arrived, they bought their tickets and went in just as anyone else."

JOHN D. ROCKEFELLER, JR., LEAVING BASSETT HALL IN COLONIAL WILLIAMSBURG, THE FAVORITE OF HIS SEVERAL HOMES.

The official Williamsburg welcome to the "Yankees from New York" was warm, too. The City Council, on December 20, 1928, dispatched a special gift to New York City—a barrel of James River oysters. The day after Christmas, Rockefeller wrote the council, "The entire family pronounced the oyster stew—which we had at the Christmas dinner—one of the best they had ever eaten." Not to be outdone, the neighboring Board of Supervisors of James City County sent a Western Union telegram to New York on December 20, 1928, announcing, "We are sending to your home by today's express a live turkey for your Christmas dinner." The next day Rockefeller announced the arrival of the big bird, telling the supervisors, "He is a beauty and worthy of the state from which he comes and of the friends who sent him." Moved by these generous exchanges, Rockefeller remarked, "People seldom give me anything." Thus, the Rockefeller enthusiasm deepened, reinforced by the genuine friendliness and hospitality of the local citizens. The Rockefellers, just as naturally, responded in many neighborly ways.

Over the years, the citizens of Williamsburg would hear from time to time of quiet benefactions to the sick or of a check dispatched to a family who had lost a member after a long and expensive illness. Soldiers stationed at nearby Fort Eustis during World War II were invited to tour Williamsburg. Some would be asked to Sunday dinner by the Rockefellers. There were stories, too, of subtle offers to save priceless storm-damaged boxwood or trees on estates whose owners no longer had the means to cope with setbacks.

Miss Elizabeth Hayes, Dr. Goodwin's secretary, following the death of her father, received this note from Rockefeller: "The expense of illness is always heavy. Will you not let me help you in bearing the burden to the extent of the enclosed check?" It was for $250.

Another time Rockefeller learned that an aged lady living on the Duke of Gloucester Street was in dire straits and was slowly removing the siding from her house to use for firewood. He quietly arranged for the lady to move to the Williamsburg Lodge at no cost for the rest of her life.

An event at Cedar Grove Cemetery further endeared Rockefeller to the populace. Quite unobtrusively he attended the funeral service and burial of a close Williamsburg neighbor. After other mourners departed from the graveyard, Rockefeller asked the mortician if he could stay "until the grave is completed." This gesture prompted another warm reaction in the community and was cited as a measure of Rockefeller's genuine compassion for Williamsburg and its citizens.

Rockefeller was also sensitive to the demands the restoration project placed on various parts of the community and made major donations to the fire and police departments, the Williamsburg Community Hospital, etc. In 1957, Rockefeller made a $500,000 gift to Bruton Parish Episcopal Church. Noting the church had been in continuous use since 1715, Rockefeller said the contribution should supplement funds the parish was spending for its ministry and music programs. He said he was "aware that no adequate understanding of the life and times of early Williamsburg is possible without the realization of the religious and spiritual aspects of this society as well evoked in Bruton."

At the same time, Rockefeller was enjoying his personal role in the restoration. He participated in the hiring of a harpsichord player for the Williamsburg Inn, in the selection of draperies and chandeliers, laundry equipment, location of warehouses, help at the hotels and

MR. AND MRS. JOHN D. ROCKEFELLER, JR., SOON AFTER
THEIR MARRIAGE IN 1901. (ROCKEFELLER ARCHIVE CENTER)

location of a filtration pool. Once he sent a note to Chorley requesting, "You get in touch with me before invitations to our next Williamsburg function are sent out. I would like very much to have a word with you as to their form."

Chorley once reported to Rockefeller that he had slipped into Raleigh Tavern to observe a new hostess at work and heard her say to a group of visitors, "This is the famous Apollo Room where Jefferson danced with his fair Belinda, where Phi Beta Kappa was founded, where Washington often dined and afterward went across the street and slept with Mrs. Campbell."

One involvement provided the New Yorker with a taste of small-town life that his background had denied him—membership in the centuries-old male gathering known as the Pulaski Club.

Reputed to be the oldest social club in America, it was founded in 1779 in honor of Revolutionary soldier Count Casimir Pulaski. The Polish nobleman visited Williamsburg briefly on April 16, 1779, en route to joining General Benjamin Lincoln in South Carolina. Pulaski was killed in the battle of Savannah in October 1779. His name was chosen for veneration, allegedly on the recommendation of General George Washington, who said, "Something should be done to commemorate Pulaski." Hence, the unnamed Williamsburg coffee klatch of the 1770s became the Pulaski Club. Because Pulaski was thirty-one when he died, the Williamsburg Pulaski Club is restricted to thirty-one members (once twenty-nine members, until the error in his age at death was discovered).

Other traditions of the carefully controlled membership are that the "initiation fee is a quart of Virginia Bourbon Whiskey" and the "membership card is written out on an Octagon Soap Wrapper." Further, "two members constitute a quorum," and the regular meeting place "is the three benches located in front of the Cole Book Shop" on Duke of Gloucester Street across from historic Bruton Parish Church. Finally, a banquet is held annually to "drink a toast to departed members and to bring in any new members. . . ." Once the group decided that a good definition of the Pulaski Club would be "a loosely-knit group of like-minded individuals who like to see things go their way."

As their background might predict, Mr. and Mrs. Rockefeller spent some of their early Williamsburg sojourns at the Episcopal rectory, located next door to the Cole Shop and adjacent to the three Pulaski Club benches near the street.

One day Rockefeller was sitting on the rectory porch, rocking gently and reading the morning newspaper. In a burst of hospitality, a Pulaskian asked the visiting New Yorker to step down and join the group's discussion of the day. Rockefeller accepted promptly. It was years later, however, that he became "one of the good old boys." As Dr. Carleton Casey, the club's archivist, said, "He just sat on the bench until there was a place for him in the club."

Rockefeller was officially admitted on November 21, 1950, during an annual dinner at Mrs. Austin's home on outlying Centerville Road. A member reported that Rockefeller "was carried away by such an honor." After the ceremony, Rockefeller said, "I know you want something, tell me what it is, and I'll see if I can provide it." R. W. Kyger, who held the triple title in the club as secretary, treasurer and sergeant-at-arms, replied, "Mr. Rockefeller, we just want you to be a member of the Pulaski Club."

"What are the dues?" Rockefeller asked.

"Four dollars," Kyger replied (probably the cost of the dinner).

Then the inevitable happened. Rockefeller felt his pockets. He didn't have any money. Embarrassed, he asked Willard Gilley for a quick loan, and the evening ended as Rockefeller paid in full—with borrowed money! Later, Rockefeller was invited to the club's annual dinner with the admonition, "As a member in good standing you are expected to attend and on time."

In reply, Rockefeller, taking the pro-feminist side, wrote:

> One of the happy results of my marriage is that Mrs. Rockefeller and I do everything possible together and are practically never separated. For so worthy a reason as this, I am sure the members of the Club will excuse my absence from the next meeting, which I regret not to attend.

He enclosed $20 for dues and "expenses of the dinner."

Rockefeller later provided three new benches for the club, and Mrs. Rockefeller commissioned an artist, John Zaharov, to paint a picture of Pulaski members sitting near the "warm stove" in the back of H. D. Cole's store, where they met on cold days. Club members wondered how Rockefeller, a teetotaler Baptist, would get around the requirement to provide a bottle of bourbon for his initiation. Adroitly, he dispatched his chauffeur with the bottle a day ahead of his induction. Winthrop, who also became a member, did not share his father's scruples and easily met the bottle test.

Out of this "special welcome" and other friendly acknowledgments, the Rockefellers were accepted completely as "real people" by the Williamsburgers.

One local newspaper, commenting on the once-strange liaison between the wealthy couple from New York and the modest citizens of Williamsburg, summed it up this way: "The Rockefellers act like Virginians, but the Virginians try to act like Rockefellers."

What endeared local citizens the most was Rockefeller's keen interest in the old town and his quiet way of moving about nearly incognito for several months each year. He sought no special recognition, favors or attention.

As the restoration work progressed, Rockefeller continued to pay rapt attention to details, vigilant that authenticity, accuracy and quality were followed to the nth degree. Once, as he was placing some of his own porcelains on a mantel in the Palace, a little old lady darted away from a tour group, yanked Rockefeller by the arm and said, "Don't you know that Mr. Rockefeller gave us these priceless things to cherish? Don't you dare touch them." Rockefeller was first so shocked and then amused he didn't say a word. He stopped "touching" until his admonisher moved to another room. Another time a carpenter told a bystander, "I wouldn't be surprised if Mr. Rockefeller himself should drop in on the job." The bystander was Rockefeller.

For the rest of his life, Rockefeller remained attentive to Williamsburg activities. Not long before he died in 1960, I saw him sitting with Mrs. Rockefeller in their well-used maroon Cadillac watching the militia practice drill on the green near the old Capitol.

The Rockefellers, devout Baptists and steady churchgoers, alternated between the Baptist, Episcopal, Methodist and Presbyterian churches when they were in Williamsburg. One Sunday, Archie Brooks, a Williamsburg native, was taking the offering at the Methodist Church. A gray-haired stranger dropped a $20 bill into the plate. Astonished at seeing so much money (far more than the total of an entire collection), Brooks, knowing the amount

THE FRIENDLY ROCKEFELLERS, WHO
ATTENDED MANY LOCAL EVENTS,
CAME TO THE OPENING OF THE
WILLIAMSBURG USO ON MAY 6, 1943.

THIS PORTRAIT OF MRS. JOHN D.
ROCKEFELLER, JR., BY ROBERT
BRACKMAN, HANGS AT THE ABBY
ALDRICH ROCKEFELLER FOLK ART
CENTER IN WILLIAMSBURG.

must be a mistake, leaned over and whispered, "Sir, didn't you make a mistake, that is $20." Rockefeller shook his head, no. Shirley Payne Low, later a key supervisor for Colonial Williamsburg's interpretive corps, reported that when her husband passed the collection plate in another church, Rockefeller frequently gave a $100 bill. At any rate, Rockefeller's Sunday donations gave the citizenry something to talk about for at least a week.

The New Yorker and his wife traditionally spent April and October, the two prettiest months, in Williamsburg. They would take the train overnight to Richmond, and a chauffeur would meet them at the Richmond station. One Sunday morning everything went wrong after the train arrived, disembarked passengers and continued south. It was fairly early, 8:00 A.M. No chauffeur appeared. Rockefeller deposited a dime in the telephone. The operator tried three different Williamsburg numbers. Alas, no one answered. The operator said she was sorry, but she would be happy to refund the dime if the caller would please give her his name and address. Mr. Rockefeller replied:

"My name is John D. . . . " He stopped there, adding, "Oh well, you wouldn't believe it anyway!" He then hung up and called a taxi for the fifty-mile trip to Williamsburg.

Years later, John Colburn, President of the Associated Press Managing Editors, was introducing Winthrop Rockefeller as the host for the APME's annual meeting being held in Williamsburg. He told the story of Winthrop's father losing the coin to the telephone company and presented him a dime. Winthrop said he was sure his father would appreciate the refund.

In the 1930s, the *Richmond Times-Dispatch* asked Rockefeller what he liked best about Williamsburg. He replied that foremost its powerful history appealed to him.

"Williamsburg has a lesson for us today," he said. "We can always learn from great men. The men of Colonial Williamsburg were individuals. They had the courage to be themselves and to do what they thought was right. That is the lesson we can learn."

Personally, Rockefeller suggested the biggest attraction of Williamsburg to him and his wife was its willingness to let them be themselves. Living in little Williamsburg, he said,

> hasn't been difficult. Most people are willing to let you be just folks. . . . Sunday Mrs. Rockefeller and I sat in front of the post office for a long time and watched the people passing by. We often do that. And we like to walk home from the movies at night. We look in the store windows and we look at the moon and the stars. You can't appreciate Williamsburg unless you walk through the town. Always you see something different: a fence or a chimney from some angle you never saw before. . . . I feel I really belong in Williamsburg. . . . Of course, your Southern charm and hospitality have meant very much. You Southerners express so graciously what the people in the North may feel just as strongly, but don't show.

Rockefeller's keen interest in Williamsburg never wavered. His extraordinary dedication promoted Goodwin to say, in summary, "The soul of Williamsburg appealed to the soul of a rare and cultured man."

BASSETT HALL, A COLONIAL HAVEN

As time passed, it became clear that the Rockefellers' ever-growing fascination with Williamsburg would lead to another kind of commitment—one reinforced by Dr. Goodwin's deft suggestion that the Rockefellers should have a Williamsburg home. On November 29, 1926, Goodwin wrote to Rockefeller, "I wish you would buy Bassett Hall for yourself. It would give you a charming vantage point from which to play with the vision and the dream. . . . " The estate of 600 acres extended from the woodlands near the Historic Area to the street adjacent to the Capitol.

Goodwin recognized quite accurately that the rich history of Bassett Hall, dating from 1750, would appeal to the Rockefellers. In back of the house stood the Great Oak—already in the 1920s, 275 years old. Goodwin knew the tree was eighty years old when Patrick Henry fought the British Stamp Act at the Capitol, barely a half-mile away. He knew that George Washington had visited Bassett Hall several times and that the estate drew its name from Burwell Bassett, a nephew of Martha Washington. As Bassett's guest in 1804, the Irish poet Thomas Moore witnessed thousands of fireflies sparkling in the woods near the house. Having never seen these winged beetles before, the poet was inspired to write "To a Firefly" at Bassett Hall (see poem at end of chapter).

The Rockefellers were astonished, too, to learn that Bassett Hall had been the scene of the most unusual North-South love story of the War between the States. During the Battle of Williamsburg, on May 5, 1862, Captain John W. Lea, a Confederate officer, was wounded and taken prisoner by the Union Army. Former West Point classmates recognized Lea and quartered him quite comfortably at Bassett Hall for his recovery. When the Union Army was planning to withdraw from Williamsburg, young Captain Custer obtained permission from General George B. McClellan to visit his former classmate, Lea. When Custer arrived, he discovered Lea was nearly recovered and, in fact, was in such good shape that he was planning to be married in about a week to Margaret Durfey, daughter of the owner of Bassett Hall.

The wedding was moved up to the following evening so Custer could stand up with Lea. Captain Lea wore his new gray Confederate uniform, attended by Captain Custer, in his blue

BASSETT HALL, WILLIAMSBURG RESIDENCE OF MR. AND MRS. JOHN D. ROCKEFELLER, JR., WAS RESTORED BY THEM FOR INFORMAL FAMILY LIVING.

MRS. ROCKEFELLER STARTED
THE FOURTEEN ACRES OF GARDENS
AT BASSETT HALL BY PLANTING
BULBS AND WILDFLOWERS UNDER
THE 300-YEAR-OLD GREAT OAK.

A WIDE STAIRCASE DOMINATES
THE ENTRANCE HALL OF THE
EIGHTEENTH-CENTURY HOUSE,
RISING IN THREE STAGES TO THE
SECOND FLOOR. THE PAINTINGS
WERE DONE DIRECTLY ON
GLASS BY CHINESE PAINTERS.

Union uniform. Elsewhere, and not too far away, the war went on full tilt—but not at this Bassett Hall "truce." In fact, Custer stayed on and the two officers played cards for ten days or so in the company of the bride and her pretty "Cousin Maggie" from Richmond. Custer wrote to his sister on September 21, 1862, that the bridegroom won every card game when the pair played for the Confederacy as the prize—"he representing the South, I the North."

After the war ended, Lea became an Episcopal rector serving parishes in West Virginia. Custer was promoted to brigadier general at age twenty-three, won military fame in the West and was killed in 1876 at the Battle of the Little Big Horn.

At any rate, Goodwin's insight triumphed, and the old estate became the Williamsburg home of the Rockefellers in 1936. Mrs. Rockefeller was ecstatic. She told a Williamsburg hostess, "Oh, I am so happy today. John has promised me we can have Bassett Hall. And he says I can keep it if I promise not to take in tourists."

The "peaceful and homelike" qualities of Bassett Hall fit the Rockefellers' tastes exceedingly well, and Mrs. Rockefeller wrote to her son David, "Our evenings . . . are always spent very peacefully here with Papa on one side of the fireplace and me on the other."

The prestigious estate also appealed to the younger Rockefellers and their wives. On November 2, 1945, Mrs. Rockefeller wrote to her sister, Lucy:

> I'm sitting in the most beautiful sunshine (at Bassett Hall), listening to a mocking bird. John and Blanchette are arriving late this afternoon . . . and then on Monday, Winthrop and Nelson are coming. Now that they are more or less their own bosses, they all seem to have a desire to come down here, which, of course, pleases John and me enormously. Sometime after the wedding, David and Peggy are coming.

Mrs. Rockefeller reveled in decorating the house with her collection of early American folk art. Rockefeller had the workmen cut a circular hole in the trees so he could stand on the front porch in the spring and see the Great Union flag of the British Empire flying over the Capitol only a block away. Thus, the Rockefellers' immersion into Williamsburg had another anchor, assuring their deepening interest in the restoration.

Rockefeller's biographer, Raymond B. Fosdick, said, "Perhaps his favorite residence—the one that most attracted him in later years—was the small white house known as Bassett Hall in Williamsburg. Here, surrounded by the vast details of a vast project, he found the satisfaction of creation, of being a part of one of his own great dreams."

Mrs. Rockefeller used Bassett Hall as a homey showcase for her ever-expanding folk art collection, which eventually spilled over into the Abby Aldrich Rockefeller Folk Art Center, now located several blocks away. But pieces still remain at Bassett Hall, which is open to the public, decorated much as it was when John and Abby were in residence.

Bassett Hall inspired Abby to counsel her sons on the value of art and, quite separately, how to behave. She wrote from her sanctuary:

> It would be a great joy to me if you did find that you had a real love for and interest in beautiful things. We could have such good times going about together, and if you start to cultivate your taste and eyes so young, you ought to be very good at it by the time you can afford to collect much. . . . To me, art is one of the great resources of my life. I feel that it enriches

the spiritual life and makes one more sane and sympathetic, more observant and understanding, as well as being good for one's nerves.

As for conduct, she recommended:

> What I would like you to do is what I try humbly to do myself: that is never to say or do anything that would wound the feelings or self-respect of any human being, and to those who are repressed, give special consideration. This is what Papa does naturally from the fineness of his nature and the kindness of his heart. I long to have our family stand firmly for what is best and highest in life. It isn't easy, but it is worthwhile.

Williamsburg didn't see Nelson, Laurance or David Rockefeller too often. First, the project was their father's prime interest. Second, directional control of the Historic Area was assigned successively to brothers John 3rd and, later, to Winthrop. Third, Nelson was deeply committed as Vice President of the United States and Governor of New York. David was dedicated to his banking and other financial interests, and Laurance dedicated his time to conservation projects and business ventures, including hotel and resort development. Therefore, their visits to Williamsburg over the years were confined largely to personal trips to Bassett Hall.

However, Nelson Rockefeller did come to Colonial Williamsburg for its fiftieth anniversary on November 27, 1976. As Nelson's private plane was late arriving at Patrick Henry International Airport, Humelsine asked me to meet Nelson. I was instructed to make one "important point." Knowing that Nelson was busy and unfamiliar with the event, Humselsine told me to explain that he would be meeting Governor Godwin and also a member of the Reverend Goodwin's family. Nelson told me abruptly that he certainly knew the difference. But when he went to the lectern to make his remarks, he began loudly, "Governor Goodwin. . . ." Humelsine never believed I really had carried out his briefing instructions!

On one occasion, Nelson came to Williamsburg as part of a political campaign. Afterward, he wrote me this letter:

NELSON A. ROCKEFELLER

June 23, 1968

Dear Don:

Thank you so much for all you did to make my far too brief visit to Williamsburg so pleasant and enjoyable. I was delighted to be in your company and appreciated greatly your escorting me through the parade grounds to the Inn.

Incidentally, I share the family pride in Williamsburg, and I do want to tell you that the members of the press traveling with me thought the buffet was just about the best ever. Ann Whitman tells me that you were formerly a member of the White House Press Corps so I suspect you realize how important after a weary week such a thing becomes. At any rate, congratulations! With much gratitude and best wishes.

Sincerely,
/s/ Nelson

THE BASSETT HALL PARLOR, MORE FORMAL THAN THE FAMILY'S MORNING ROOM, HAS ENGLISH FURNITURE "IN THE FRENCH TASTE."

On another visit, Nelson asked to see the Abby Aldrich Rockefeller Folk Art Collection, named after his mother. After touring the building, he asked, "Where are Mother's things?" He was told other folk art items were brought in from time to time for exhibition. He was not pleased, and it wasn't long after his visit that the "Collection" became the Abby Aldrich Rockefeller Folk Art "Center." His mother's collection is housed in the main building while other functions are in a related building.

Of all the Williamsburg people the Rockefellers met they regarded none more highly than their "fence neighbors" at Bassett Hall, the three Morecock sisters, Elizabeth (Pinky), Kathryn (Kitty) and Agnes. As time passed, some ticklish neighborhood matters came up that had to be dealt with judiciously and delicately. For example, the Morecock sisters' chickens took an annoying fancy to the Rockefellers' yard. Also, two cherry trees and a locust stump that Rockefeller wanted removed were straddling the property lines. Rockefeller wisely took up the matter with Colonial Williamsburg President Kenneth Chorley and Vernon M. Geddy, local attorney and Executive Vice President of Colonial Williamsburg. At all costs, Rockefeller told Chorley and Geddy, the chickens, trees and stump mission was to be accomplished "without at all affecting the warm relations which have always existed between the Misses Morecock and ourselves and which we so highly value." Because of his local background, Geddy was sent to negotiate with the sisters. He did a masterful job, reporting to Chorley on March 13, 1944, as follows:

I have just come back from a very delightful interview with Miss Kitty Morecock. As I told you over the telephone this morning, after getting all of the information from Mr. Brouwers, Mr. Lavery and Mr. Kendrew, I made a date with Miss Pinky Morecock and took her in the car and showed her the two cherry trees and the locust stump that we wanted to cut down and told her about our willingness to erect a chicken yard so that Miss Kitty could keep her chickens in it. Miss Pinky was very appreciative of our willingness to help Miss Kitty keep her chickens in and said she would pave the way for me with Kitty. Saturday Miss Pinky called me and told me that she thought Miss Kitty was in a very pleasant mood now and suggested that I go to see her about the details. When I went to see her this afternoon she could not have been nicer and I am sure

THE DINING ROOM WAS CONSIDERED THE MOST PLEASANT ROOM OF ALL
BY MRS. ROCKEFELLER. FROM HERE SHE SAW THE SUN SET BEHIND THE GARDEN.

she is a very sincere admirer of Mr. and Mrs. Rockefeller. She was most appreciative of our offer to fix her chicken yard and she told me I could cut down the two cherry trees and the stump.

You might also tell Mr. Rockefeller that the Committee on Diplomacy was required, before leaving the Morecock household, to drink one old fashioned made with rum and then as Kitty said, "Before we cut the cherry tree down we have got to drink a glass of cherry bounce." For the good of the cause your committee did both and in addition ate several cookies, and came out bouncing but with the bacon.

I immediately got in touch with Ed Kendrew and he is going to fix up the chicken yard right away and have the trees taken away.

V.M.G.

There is a friendly but grim epilogue to the chicken episode. One errant fowl persisted in escaping from the pen. Finally captured, the chicken paid with its life. In the good neighbor spirit, the Morecock sisters baked the chicken and delivered it to the Rockefellers!

IN THE MASTER BEDROOM MRS. ROCKEFELLER USED A VARIETY OF PINKS SUCH AS THOSE IN THE FIGURINES, THE HOOKED RUG AND THE COUCH.

HER LARGE FOLK ART COLLECTION OUTGREW HER HOME AND IS NOW IN THE
ABBY ALDRICH FOLK ART CENTER, WHICH INCLUDES THIS STENCILED WALL GALLERY.

However, this did not solve all the fowl problems between the two properties. The next issue requiring deft diplomacy involved the Morecocks' roving pet guinea hens.

Rockefeller's bedroom was on the south side of Bassett Hall. In the mornings he would arise, walk to the window, check the thermometer and decide what suit he would wear. There were too many days, however, when he was awakened early by the cry and chatter of the invading guineas perched in the trees near his window. Finally, the distraction reached the point where Rockefeller called in Chorley and Kendrew for advice, cautioning again that the problem was to be handled with the utmost finesse.

After some hush-hush, high-level meetings it was suggested to the ladies that the chickens might appreciate a canopy over the new chicken yard to provide shade. The sisters may have suspected some ulterior motive was lurking "under the canopy" when it was mentioned casually that the guineas might also enjoy "the shade." The ladies agreed to the proposal, but soon several guineas out-smarted the strategists and decided to move over to the Rockefellers' yard.

What to do?

Kendrew recalls that the Morecocks finally realized that the four "escapees had to be eliminated." The ultimate solution, however, becomes hazy in the pages of Williamsburg history.

"I don't know who did it," Kendrew said. "But one Sunday morning, I was invited to the Morecock house, and they presented me with four beautifully roasted guinea hens for our Sunday dinner. I have no way of knowing for sure if they were the birds that bothered Mr. Rockefeller. At any rate, they were never seen again."

Five years later, following Mrs. Rockefeller's death, Rockefeller asked Geddy to approach the Morecock ladies and propose a memorial to his late wife in the form of "a little fund" for each of the Morecocks to add to their "sense of security." His offer was accepted, funds were provided through securities, and a year later Rockefeller wrote his "Dear Friends" and forwarded additional securities, i.e., forty shares of Standard Oil and twenty-five shares of the Ohio Oil Company. He added more securities to the "little fund" the following year.

Despite neighborhood distractions, the Rockefellers made certain they did not overlook The College of William and Mary, another of their Williamsburg neighbors. Among other personal entertaining, Mr. and Mrs. Rockefeller would invite six students from time to time for afternoon tea at Bassett Hall.

One British student, Jack Morpurgo, class of 1938, recalled that college authorities specified that students be "clean—clean suit, clean shirt, hair cut, shoes shined" before going to Bassett Hall to meet the Rockefellers.

"Later on in life, I was invited to Buckingham Palace with far fewer instructions," Morpurgo said.

Shortly before she died of a heart condition in April 1948, Mrs. Rockefeller restated her love for Bassett Hall: "I would like to stay on for a month longer. It is so peaceful and quiet and the lack of excitement keeps my blood pressure from soaring to the skies."

In 1951, Rockefeller married Martha Baird Allen, widow of his classmate at Brown University, and they continued to visit Bassett Hall regularly until Rockefeller died in 1960.

To a Firefly
By Thomas Moore
(Written at Bassett Hall)

At morning when the earth and sky
Are glowing with the light of spring
We see thee not, thou humble fly
Nor think upon thy gleaming wing.
But when the skies have lost their hue,
And sunny lights no longer play,
Or then we see and bless thee, too,
For sparkling o'er the dreary way.
Then let me hope, when lost to me
The lights that now my life illume
Some milder joys may come like thee
To cheer, if not to warm, the gloom.

FROM FATHER TO SON TO SON

In 1953, extraordinary events in the Rockefeller family triggered an unprecedented shifting of authority at Colonial Williamsburg, followed by a period of unsettled direction. When family decisions were finally determined, after hard and sometimes tense debates, a dramatic phase of expansion occurred in property and in the restoration's educational and interpretive programs.

Until 1952, John D. Rockefeller 3rd had been his father's clear choice to head the Colonial Williamsburg Board of Trustees, and he had, therefore, assumed the role of Chairman in 1941. In 1948, John 3rd and his wife, Blanchette, acquired Bassett Hall but only for their future use. His mother, Abby, had bequeathed the house furnishings to the younger Rockefellers, and the elder Rockefellers soon turned over the deed to Bassett Hall to them, subject to their life use. The transfer of power was moving smoothly inside the tight confines of the family.

All went well until early 1952 when John D. Rockefeller, Jr., and his son unexpectedly met head-on in their differences over how Colonial Williamsburg was to view its mission in the future. Father and son met three times between January 6 and 11, 1952, to attempt to reconcile their impasse. Thereafter, John 3rd summarized the Williamsburg problem in these words in his diary:

> As a result of these talks it became increasingly clear that Father wasn't happy at the thought of Williamsburg becoming the focal point of a democracy-citizenship program of a broader character; that his conception seemed to be that Williamsburg was an end, not its being a means to an end, as I had conceived it. Father specifically indicated that his thought as to an educational program was limited to two things; first, making a visit to Colonial Williamsburg as inspirational as possible and, secondly, only carrying on such educational activities outside Williamsburg as would encourage people to visit Williamsburg.

That was it. The younger Rockefeller said in frustration, "If I had realized what I know now, I would not have gone back into the Williamsburg picture following the war." After a decent

GATHERED AT THE WEDDING OF WINTHROP PAUL ROCKEFELLER AND DEBORAH SAGE AT BRUTON PARISH WERE THE FOUR BROTHERS (FROM LEFT): NELSON, WINTHROP, JOHN D. 3RD AND LAURANCE. AT UPPER LEFT ARE DAVID ROCKEFELLER, JR., AND JOHN ROCKEFELLER IV.

interval following the very uncharacteristic dispute, John 3rd resigned at the end of 1952 as Chairman of the Board of Trustees of Colonial Williamsburg.

This conflict was the one Winthrop had alluded to when he and I met at Washington National Airport in early 1958. It was not a pleasant situation but the intra-Rockefeller dispute cleared the way for Winthrop to become Chairman in 1953. Under his supervision, operations moved along smoothly, and two years later, Rockefeller, Jr., now past eighty years of age, stepped aside from all responsibilities, saying to the Trustees, " . . . I have high hopes for Colonial Williamsburg. It is with the fullest confidence in you that the mantle of my responsibility has fallen on your shoulders." Winthrop was present on this occasion.

When Rockefeller died on May 11, 1960, Winthrop was clearly in charge. With Humelsine's counsel, backed by the Board of Trustees, Winthrop avoided grappling with details, but he left no doubt that Colonial Williamsburg's future was a prime responsibility on his agenda. In private talks, he emphasized his keen interest in undertaking more projects that would bear his own label while complementing his late father's earlier work and interests. On many occasions he flew from his Arkansas ranch to escort VIPs from abroad around the Historic Area.

Win was not reticent about expressing his interest in the revival and advancement of Williamsburg's eighteenth-century role in fashioning a new form of democracy for the young republic.

In fact, Rockefeller was forthright in publicizing his chairmanship of Colonial Williamsburg in his campaigns for the governorship of Arkansas in 1964 and 1966. His key campaign document, "The Win Rockefeller Story," distributed throughout the state, listed forty-four achievements and interests. On the list his military service record was first. Second was Colonial Williamsburg, depicted this way:

> As most Americans know, the most ambitious restoration project ever undertaken in America is the rebuilding of Colonial Williamsburg, the early capital of Virginia. The original idea and impetus came from Winthrop's father, John D. Rockefeller, Jr., . . . so that the future may learn from the past.
>
> Winthrop Rockefeller, in the years he has devoted to this ever-growing project, feels he has learned a great deal from seeing history brought to life so that young and old may learn more about the ways of life of the men who started our nation.
>
> He also feels he has learned in Williamsburg many practical things about the travel and tourist industry. Williamsburg is now one of the major tourist attractions of America.

Previously Winthrop had heard from Humelsine that the organization's long search for a nearby plantation might be realized if Carter's Grove, only eight miles away, could be purchased. Win was surprised but fascinated with the possibility. This could be his big project. His father had once negotiated unsuccessfully for historic Shirley Plantation, more than twenty miles from Williamsburg up the James River. Failing that, Colonial Williamsburg in 1953 purchased Kingsmill Plantation as the possible site for portraying plantation life, adding another dimension to a trip to Williamsburg. Kingsmill was only four miles from the Historic Area, but its mansion had been destroyed, leaving only two eighteenth-century

MR. AND MRS. WINTHROP ROCKEFELLER, CHAIRMAN OF THE BOARD OF TRUSTEES, AND
PRESIDENT AND MRS. CARLISLE H. HUMELSINE IN 1968.

OVERLOOKING THE JAMES RIVER, THE EIGHTEENTH-CENTURY MANSION
AT CARTER'S GROVE IS NOW OWNED BY COLONIAL WILLIAMSBURG.

flanking buildings as colonial survivors. The goal had always been to secure an original eighteenth-century mansion to show and interpret to visitors.

When the chatelaine of Carter's Grove, Mary C. "Molly" McCrea, died in 1960 her will stated her desire that the plantation of 800 acres on the James River and the handsome, large brick mansion dating to the 1750s be sold. She also suggested that the property be acquired by "some association or foundation that would protect this outstanding example of Virginia colonial architecture" and open it to "interested persons," i.e., the public.

The signal was clear. Colonial Williamsburg was virtually the only "association or foundation" capable of purchasing the valuable property. Therefore, negotiations began, and in 1963 Sealantic Fund, a Rockefeller philanthropic organization, with Winthrop happily guiding the purchase, acquired the property. Colonial Williamsburg was assigned to operate Carter's Grove. It was opened to the public in 1964 and conveyed to Colonial Williamsburg in 1969.

Carter's Grove was no ordinary acquisition. The estate was rich in colonial history, and Mrs. McCrea enhanced its mystique during her stewardship from 1928 to 1960. She had the roof raised on the main house, added dormers to create living space on the third floor and connected two dependencies creating a single, sprawling, country home in the English tradition. The result was described by architectural historian Samuel Chamberlain as "the most beautiful house in America."

The *New York Times* described the mansion and its setting as replete with "manicured Georgian gardens and crushed oyster-shell pathways, a beautiful house with brass chandeliers, formal dining room, black walnut staircase and gilt-framed paintings."

Winthrop laughed when Humelsine, who had been invited to the plantation while he was a World War II soldier at nearby Fort Eustis, recalled this story as told by his hostess, Mrs. McCrea (who made no bones about her preference for men instead of women at her social affairs). She said:

> I met Mr. McCrea this way . . . I was a widow and not knowing what to do decided to go to the Greenbrier Hotel for a rest. As I walked down the hall from my room to go to dinner the first evening, I saw outside a room this enormous pair of men's white shoes waiting to be polished during the night. I made a note of the room number and diplomatically determined that the room was occupied by a widower, one Archibald M. McCrea who, I found out, was a prominent Pittsburgh industrialist and son of the president of the Pennsylvania Railroad! With this information, I made up my mind that any man who could fill those large white shoes could be my husband. On the second night of my stay, I had dinner with Mr. McCrea.

At any rate, Carter's Grove was a tremendous coup, public and personal. Not only did it enjoy a reputation as one of the outstanding historic plantations, but Winthrop himself had been able to bring to fruition one of his father's dreams. The fact that he had been the major force behind the acquisition represented a major and dramatic addition of Winthrop's own to the restoration program. It also whetted his growing interest in Williamsburg.

The romanticism and charisma of Carter's Grove were enhanced by legends from its two hundred years of history. Colonel Banastre Tarleton, a famous English cavalryman in the Virginia campaigns of 1781, was said to have spurred his trusty horse up the broad stairs, slashing the hand rail with his saber. Fact or fiction, the rail does have some sizeable nicks in its surface, noticeable even today. George Washington and Thomas Jefferson were said to have been refused marriage proposals made at Carter's Grove to two very eligible young ladies, Mary Cary and Rebecca Burwell. Mrs. McCrea, during her regime, had always referred to the southwest parlor as the Refusal Room.

As Carter's Grove became increasingly known as Winthrop's "statement," he started a flow of gifts totaling about $8.5 million for various projects including a private eight-mile road linking the Historic Area to the plantation, and he set up the down payment of $724,274 made by Sealantic. Everything seemed to go right. Additionally, Carter's Grove was folded into Colonial Williamsburg's administration, thus reducing the operating budget of the plantation.

Ivor Noël Hume, the restoration's archaeologist, unearthed the site of a major English settlement between the mansion and the river. Known as Martin's Hundred, the site dated back to 1620 and, among other things, contained two knight-like helmets associated with European cavalrymen in the sixteenth and seventeenth centuries. These were the first closed helmets to be discovered in the New World. These finds prompted two articles in the *National Geographic* by Noël Hume on Carter's Grove and Martin's Hundred. The National Geographic Society contributed about $250,000 in support of the five-year archaeology project.

While Carter's Grove prospered, additional important buildings were opened to the public in the Historic Area in 1968 after many years of planning, restoration and furnishing. Visitors now could see better how colonial citizens had lived. One significant house, located on Market Square, had been lived in by Peyton Randolph. Dating back to 1715, this was the home of Randolph when he was Speaker of the House of Burgesses and President of the First Continental Congress. The James Geddy House, dated 1737, was opened along with an adjacent silversmith workshop and kitchen. On the Duke of Gloucester Street, visitors came again to the 1743 Wetherburn's Tavern. In addition, six rooms were interpreted for the first time at the 1695 Wren Building at The College of William and Mary, and the McKenzie Apothecary, located near the Governor's Palace, also opened to the public.

Finally, in this Winthrop Rockefeller period Colonial Williamsburg entered into an agreement to sell the Kingsmill tract to Anheuser-Busch. As one of three participants for Colonial Williamsburg in the transaction, I saw the property as part of a corridor to Carter's Grove. This covered a huge area of 5,000 combined acres with two miles of highway frontage and a railroad on the north and four miles of deep-channel in the James River on the south. Half of the 5,000 acres had been purchased years before by Colonial Williamsburg from Tom Brooks, prominent Carolina and Virginia lumberman. Brooks had put a price of $500,000 on the 2,500 acres and would not budge a dollar. However, when the transaction was finally completed, Brooks immediately contributed $50,000 to Colonial Williamsburg.

Initially Anheuser-Busch attempted to buy property elsewhere, on the west side of Williamsburg. Humelsine was then head of the commission planning the nation's bicentennial. One day he and I were at a meeting in the State Department in Washington, D.C., when Humelsine received word that Winthrop was calling from Little Rock. Humelsine asked me to leave the meeting with him.

Winthrop said August Busch, Jr., was in his office, paying a courtesy call to say his corporation planned a business-residential development to the east of Williamsburg in the New-port News area. This was news to us; we had not heard of any plans to switch from property already being packaged for Busch on the west side of Williamsburg. When Humelsine contested Rockefeller's identification of the new area, Winthrop said, "Look, I know the areas around Williamsburg. Gussie is planning to build to the east near Newport News." He then said, "It is too bad the Kingsmill tract couldn't be sold to Busch." Because of the Rocke-feller-Busch friendship—and some failed test borings—the Newport News negotiations terminated, and Kingsmill was sold to Anheuser-Busch for more than $2 million in 1969. Humelsine said the new money would be added to Colonial Williamsburg's endowment fund, and the income "will be used to assist in the development of Carter's Grove."

The Kingsmill negotiations were up-and-down but always fascinating. Once, as part of the final settlement, Colonial Williamsburg momentarily "owned" an apartment house complex in Atlanta! It was quickly transferred to local-area owners, Meredith W. Abbitt and Caleb D. West, who sought the apartment as an important part of their side of the overall sale that eventually included property for an amusement park and a brewery. As the sale progressed, I found myself on Budweiser airplanes and in the office of the Governor of Virginia with Humelsine and Duncan M. Cocke, who preceded me as Senior Vice President of Colonial Williamsburg. Another time, we were on Busch's 120-foot yacht, floating down the James River, dining with the elder Busch and Winthrop. The Busch yacht had a large pillow on the fantail of the luxury "ship" that gave me a new appreciation of wealth. The well-known quote embroidered on the pillow read:

The difference between men and boys
is the price of their toys.

Later that evening, I began to prowl the yacht, visiting, among other areas, the bar, which extended from one side of the vessel to the other. On the back bar was a ceramic model of a Budweiser beer wagon, six horses, a driver and the familiar spotted dog. For some idle reason, I asked the veteran bartender, "What do they do with those Clydesdale horses when they become old?" The response was quick and definite:

"They send 'em over to Schlitz to make beer!"

Winthrop's interest in Williamsburg and the estate at Carter's Grove was underlined later when Bruton Parish Church was chosen as the site of the March 22, 1971, wedding of Winthrop Paul Rockefeller, son of Winthrop and Barbara Sears (Bobo) Rockefeller to Deb-orah Cluett Sage of London and New York City. All of the Rockefeller family attended except David, Sr., who was in the Far East. The event at Bruton Parish Church provided a photographer's field day for tourists. During the departure from the church, a little girl asked:

"Why are we standing here, Mommy?"

"To see *all* the Rockefellers," was the reply.

"Who are the Rockefellers?"

"They're people with lots of money who do good things with it—like here in Williamsburg."

We left the church to go to the reception in the Virginia Room of the Williamsburg Lodge.

A RARE PORTRAIT OF THE SIX ROCKEFELLER CHILDREN TAKEN SOON AFTER THEIR
FATHER'S DEATH IN 1960: JOHN D. 3RD, WINTHROP, ABBY, LAURANCE, DAVID AND
NELSON. (ROCKEFELLER ARCHIVE CENTER, PHOTO BY EZRA STOLLER © ESTO)

When Winthrop clinked his glass for quiet, we wondered how he'd handle the awkward situation: The bride's parents were divorced, as were the groom's, and there had been several remarriages. Further, Winthrop's two ex-wives, Bobo and Jeannette, were in the audience.

Win's comment on the fractured scene came forth in his usual candid manner.

"Well," he said as he introduced the family members of both sides of the newlyweds, "this reminds me of the committee that invented the camel."

The audience roared, applauded and pursued the champagne.

Because of Winthrop's interest, Carter's Grove has recently become another chapter in a long Rockefeller history of assisting minorities, especially blacks, to learn about their history and to improve the quality of their lives. As part of an unusual Colonial Williamsburg program to acknowledge colonial slavery, three eighteenth-century slave dwellings and related interpretations are now provided for visitors at Carter's Grove. Rex Ellis, a black interpreter of African-American history, states, "The subject of slavery is certainly painful, which is one of the reasons it needs to be dealt with. We need to learn from all of history, including the uncomfortable parts of history."

Winthrop was to play a key role again in shaping the future of Colonial Williamsburg and its affiliate, Carter's Grove Plantation. After he died in 1973 at age sixty-one, the trustees of Winthrop's estate followed his wishes in providing funds for the eight-mile country road from Williamsburg to Carter's Grove, for construction of a reception center at the plantation and for an archaeological museum to be named for Winthrop Rockefeller.

I have always been touched when I visit the reception center and walk down the path to a certain point of land. There stands a plaque that reads:

THIS SITE IS DEDICATED
TO THE MEMORY OF
WINTHROP ROCKEFELLER
1912—1973
CHAIRMAN OF THE BOARD OF
THE COLONIAL WILLIAMSBURG FOUNDATION
1953—1973
FRIEND, SUPPORTER AND BENEFACTOR OF
CARTER'S GROVE PLANTATION

And what doth the Lord require of thee
but to do justly, and to love mercy, and
to walk humbly with thy God?

MICAH 6:8

This memorial to his mother's favorite Bible passage and to her philosophy is yet another of Winthrop's many legacies to Williamsburg.

With Virginia Governor Linwood Holton, the Humelsines and William Reynolds, Jr., Mary and I flew to Petit Jean Mountain, Arkansas, Winthrop's "Winrock" home, for his memorial service on March 4, 1973. Sixty members of the Rockefeller family attended. The narrow runway and airport at Winrock provided parking area for only a few planes. After landing the large Reynolds Metals Company jet, the pilots had to join other planes in flying to Little Rock until the service was concluded.

Speaking for the family, New York Governor Nelson Rockefeller recalled that during Win's early life he used a magnifying glass and the sun's rays to burn the last lines of an Edgar Guest poem into a wooden plaque:

> *He started to sing*
> *As he tackled one thing*
> *That couldn't be done,*
> *And he did it.*

Nelson, in a gripping epitaph, recounted how Winthrop enlisted in the United States Army as a private a year before Pearl Harbor was attacked. During the invasion of Okinawa, a Japanese kamikaze plane hit the troop ship carrying Winthrop and his fellow fighters. All officers senior to Rockefeller were killed.

> Win immediately took command—organizing the men, restoring order, putting out the fires, and caring for the wounded until relief arrived twenty hours later. He was hospitalized for weeks afterward, but he went back to active duty again before the war ended.
>
> It's no wonder that during those war years, Win was known affectionately among the men in his outfit as "Brother Rock."

At the conclusion of the memorial service, I slipped away and walked down to the hangar covering Winthrop's three airplanes: a little tail-dragger gadfly for two that could land on farm fields; the eight-passenger King Air once used for political campaigning and other Arkansas-area flights; and the larger Falcon jet, Winthrop's pride and joy, built in France and flown to the United States where all instruments were replaced with the finest American ones. Except for the sporadic chattering of nesting sparrows, the hangar had the stillness of a morgue. Standing beside the big jet and wondering what the fate of the three planes would be, and assessing the aviation investment alone and ever, ever so much more—alerted me suddenly to the vacuum Winthrop's death left in the lives of his friends, colleagues and employees. To me personally his passing brought to an end our enjoyment of our mutual interest in aviation and journalism, two subjects that had always come up when we met alone.

I turned and walked back to the visitors' area of the Winrock cattle barn where people were gathering. By chance I arrived at the reception table just a few steps behind John D. Rockfeller 3rd. I recognized Billy Sparks, who had worked for many years at the main house, starting off Winthrop's days by taking him his breakfast. John asked Billy for a Scotch and soda.

"Mr. Rockefeller," Billy said, "all's we got is Catawba juice."

Taken completely aback by this news, Rockefeller turned toward me in total disbelief and commented, "My brother is turning over in his grave."

"I know what you mean," I replied.

NELSON ROCKEFELLER, THE NATION'S VICE PRESIDENT AT THE TIME,
STROLLS PAST BRUTON PARISH CHURCH WITH MRS. ROCKEFELLER.

PROVIDING THE FINANCIAL BACKBONE

Despite world events, observers were fascinated over the years by John D. Rockefeller, Jr.'s consistent support of the huge restoration project. Rockefeller noted in a letter to President Kenneth Chorley on October 21, 1943, that because of the war Williamsburg's gardens, greens and buildings had been neglected and that the Historic Area would require extensive renovation, rehabilitation, overhauling, replanting, etc. Rockefeller saw the end of the war as an opportunity to move ahead, and he was ready to go at it again on the pattern he had once described:

> The restoration of Williamsburg . . . offered an opportunity to restore a complete area and free it entirely from alien and inharmonious surroundings, as well as to preserve the beauty and charm of the old buildings and gardens of the city and its historic significance. Thus, it made a unique and irresistible appeal.

Then, he added:

> as the work has progressed I have come to feel that perhaps an even greater value is the lesson that it teaches of the patriotism, high purpose, and unselfish devotion of our forefathers to the common good.

Thus Rockefeller re-dedicated himself to his earlier dream, inspired by Goodwin.

> These war years have not only confirmed, but greatly increased my belief in the value to the nation of Williamsburg, both as an historic shrine without equal and as an inspiration to patriotism and to the emulation of the great men among the founders of our country who lived in or frequented Williamsburg in the early days.
>
> In the light of the above, it has been borne in upon me as I have personally been in residence in Williamsburg for weeks at a time during these war days that there was perhaps no single contribution which I could make to the rebirth of our nation that would be as far-reaching in its results as the provision of such further funds as may be necessary to carry the restoration to its completion. With that in mind I am handing you herewith as a gift to Colonial

MOTORING WAS A FAVORITE FAMILY PASTIME. HERE FATHER TAKES MOTHER FOR A SPIN IN A 1908 ELECTRIC CAR. (ROCKEFELLER ARCHIVE CENTER)

Williamsburg, Inc., the securities listed below to which I shall hope to add as I find it convenient until what seems to me an adequate total has been provided. The securities are:

Standard Oil Company of Indiana	7,100 shares
Standard Oil Company of California	16,100 shares
Standard Oil Company of New Jersey	19,000 shares
Socony Vacuum Oil Company	46,300 shares

Very sincerely,
/s/ John D. Rockefeller, Jr.

The 88,500 shares of stock were worth $2,589,875 at the time of the 1943 transaction, a fraction of what their value is today.

Again, in 1952, Rockefeller reaffirmed his commitment to the long-range financial health of Colonial Williamsburg. Never one to force progress but always quick to watch and analyze standards of quality, he raised a question about Colonial Williamsburg's operations during one of his twice-yearly (April and October) visits to Williamsburg.

In essence, the question was this: We have been subsidizing this program heavily. Should we continue this subsidy? If the Williamsburg experience is worthwhile to visitors would they pay a larger share of the cost? Could the budget be balanced? Could we operate on a break-even basis?

Chorley and his associates endorsed the idea of a self-supporting Williamsburg and went to work to cut costs, increase prices—whatever was needed to attain a break-even budget.

Rockefeller returned to Williamsburg months later and made a personal tour of the area. Then he went to the Goodwin Building, which housed the headquarters of the restoration, to check on progress, if any, toward the agreed goal.

Chorley told Rockefeller that the American people were, indeed, willing to pay more of the costs and that, in his opinion, the budget would be balanced very soon.

After expressing his pleasure at the rapid turn of events, Rockefeller digressed and asked about some specific operations which, to him, were below the usual Williamsburg standards. One of his points concerned the care of the gardens and the condition of the pachysandra at Bassett Hall. Chorley conceded that some "shortcuts" had been taken to trim the budget and that maintaining the pachysandra was one of them.

Rockefeller didn't say much more that day. He went back to Bassett Hall and reflected on the situation. Soon he communicated his decision to contribute $15 million more to be known as the Enrichment Fund. He was deeply moved by the support of visitors and, typically, said he didn't want any more shortcuts. His decision was to return the operation of Colonial Williamsburg to a subsidized basis, one that still exists today through income from endowment, hotels and restaurants, the Colonial Williamsburg reproductions program, business properties and gifts from contributors to Colonial Williamsburg.

In a letter dated April 10, 1952, Rockefeller revealed his $15 million pledge, adding, "The principal as well as the income of this gift is available wholly in your discretion for any of your corporate purposes or uses." This was the largest single gift Rockefeller had ever made to Colonial Williamsburg.

MR. AND MRS. JOHN D. ROCKEFELLER, JR., ATTEND A DANCE AT THE
WILLIAMSBURG INN, 1944. (ROCKEFELLER ARCHIVE CENTER)

Through this major new infusion of funds (based on the decision that Colonial Williamsburg should have educational, interpretive and preservation programs and other resources well beyond income provided by visitors), Rockefeller established a significant principle that makes Colonial Williamsburg an outstanding educational experience today. To augment his $15 million gift, Rockefeller freed all of his previous donations "from any conditions attaching to the use of either income or the principal thereof."

In Chorley's view, Rockefeller "turned Colonial Williamsburg loose—as a separate and individual organization" and expected it to stand on its own without Rockefeller or other outside pressures. Rockefeller's contributions to Colonial Williamsburg were never tied in any way to financial return to him or anyone in his family or to his colleagues. The Rockefellers, in other words, never received a cent in return for contributing nearly $100 million to Colonial Williamsburg.

One day, I received a telephone call from a Williamsburg reporter who asked for the "total amount of dollars the Rockefellers have contributed to projects in the Commonwealth of Virginia, including Colonial Williamsburg." It never occurred to me I could not obtain the answer, but I did ask "for a day or two." I called Rockefeller headquarters at 30 Rockefeller Plaza in New York. A day later, the answer came back, "We have no idea of the amount; we don't keep those kinds of records." My admiration for this remarkable family went up a giant notch with that response. It was only some years later that financial officers at Colonial Williamsburg arrived at the estimated $100 million mentioned above.

His quiet life in Williamsburg, his deep personal interest in the details of the restoration, his willingness to boost it financially, all made Williamsburg a special jewel to Rockefeller, notwithstanding all of his other benefactions throughout the world.

As Rockefeller's contribution grew, the Commonwealth of Virginia became more and more grateful to the New Yorker. Colonial Williamsburg as the eighteenth-century capital drew more and more national and world attention—as well as income from tax dollars. On Colonial Williamsburg's fiftieth anniversary in November 1976, Nelson Rockefeller, former Vice President of the United States and Governor of the State of New York, spoke of his father's interest in Williamsburg in this way:

> Of all the interests Father ever had, I never saw his eyes light up more or his voice take on greater excitement than when he spoke of the progress at Williamsburg. Further, I don't think that anything ever happened in Father's lifetime that meant as much to him as the fact that the great State of Virginia made him an honorary citizen and that only the Marquis de Lafayette had been so honored by the Commonwealth. This was the most significant honor he ever received.

All of Williamsburg was saddened to hear on May 11, 1960, that the old town's number-one transplanted citizen and benefactor had died in Tucson, Arizona, at age eighty-six.

In his role as President of Colonial Williamsburg, Carlisle H. Humelsine said:

> Mr. Rockefeller was not only Williamsburg's benefactor, but also its warm-hearted friend and neighbor. His devotion to the restoration of Williamsburg symbolized his deep-rooted interest in America's heritage and the spiritual and educational welfare of its citizens.
>
> As his custodians, we of Colonial Williamsburg pledge ourselves to help perpetuate as best

we can the remarkable work made possible by his foresight and high-principled patriotism. I know we all share this determination to carry on in his spirit.

A memorial service was held at Bassett Hall on June 9, 1960. The community was invited and attended in large numbers. Colonial Williamsburg employees in their workaday costumes joined in the memorial as all Historic Area buildings were closed by mid-afternoon. A community choir, the Williamsburg Quintet, and those attending—3,000 strong—sang Rockefeller's favorite hymns. The site was at the Great Oak, where Rockefeller nearly thirty-five years before had heard Dr. Goodwin outline his dreams of a restored Williamsburg. Dr. Raymond Fosdick spoke at the service of his memories of John D. Rockefeller, Jr., and his devotion to Williamsburg. He said that Rockefeller

> loved every square foot of it; and I suspect he measured every square foot of it too—with that four-foot rule which he habitually carried in his hip pocket. A lasting impression I have of him is of a very eager man down on the floor of the sitting room at Bassett Hall, surrounded by blueprints, and trying to explain to my untutored eye just what they meant. It is significant that the last letter he wrote, two days before he died, had to do with Williamsburg.

Dr. Fosdick continued:

> I like to think of him, sitting outside the little summerhouse here at the end of the path, and looking across the boxwoods at this giant oak tree. "It is a place to sit in silence and let the past speak to us," he once said. And surely this oak can speak to those whose ears are attuned to its voice. It tells us of a glorious past—a story of great men, of great courage, of the gallantry and high faith of those who went before us. And it tells us, too, of a twentieth-century man who wanted nothing for himself, a man of simplicity and dignity, a man who asked only for the opportunity of restoring the past to the present and to the future, so that its inspiration and its beauty might live again.

As the memorial service concluded, it was clear that although the benefactor of Williamsburg was gone, he had left a major legacy of spirit and money that gave his prized project a strong inspirational and financial backbone. But there was a nagging question: Had Rockefeller provided enough funds to guarantee Colonial Williamsburg's future?

ROCKEFELLERS TO READER'S DIGEST
TO THE FUTURE

When Rockefeller died in 1960, his personal benefactions to Williamsburg totaled $68,348,354—nearly fifteen times what he had estimated in the beginning as the absolute maximum the project would cost him. This amount had seemed adequate at the time, but when Winthrop Rockefeller died in 1973, and with a turndown in the national economy and an accompanying oil crisis that curbed vacation travel, it became clear that new sources of funding, probably from the public sector, would be required. Certainly, no one family in the years ahead could support any institution the size of Colonial Williamsburg and keep costs within the range of most travelers. Nevertheless, the Rockefeller family's support after John D. Rockefeller, Jr.'s death, continued. By the end of 1989, various Rockefeller family members and family-sponsored foundations and trusts had increased total Rockefeller contributions to a whopping $99,675,932, including Rockefeller, Jr.'s nearly $70 million. Any university, college, religious or other institution would have welcomed such support, especially from one source.

A transition from solely Rockefeller support to a wide variety of funding began in 1976, through the unerring intuition of Carlisle H. Humelsine, who forecast the need for a financial development program. As President of Colonial Williamsburg, Humelsine initiated a fund-raising development program and hired F. Roger Thaler, from Duke University, to head it. Thaler was a professional fund-raiser and a lawyer who also received the executive support of Humelsine's successor, Charles R. Longsworth.

During this planning phase, Mike Radock, Vice President for University Relations at the University of Michigan, was called in to make a three-day feasibility study. He was asked a big question: Could an institution, such as Colonial Williamsburg, so closely tied for fifty years to the Rockefeller name, hope to attract funds from individuals, corporations and foundations? We doubted it could. Radock's answer was unequivocal and a surprise to us. "The name of Rockefeller," he said, "will be an asset. People will want to associate with the name and with Colonial Williamsburg."

Radock could not have been more right.

LILA AND DEWITT WALLACE, CO-FOUNDERS OF *READER'S DIGEST*, WERE FREQUENT
VISITORS AND MAJOR CONTRIBUTORS TO COLONIAL WILLIAMSBURG.

Under Thaler's leadership, backed by Humelsine's and Longsworth's support, the amount raised between 1976 and 1990 totaled $103 million in gifts and pledges. Gifts, grants and pledges totaled $12.9 million in 1989 alone.

In addition to the gifts, through wise investments and fund-raising, the restoration organization had an endowment fund whose market value, in the fall of 1990, had reached about $170 million. The annual income from an amount of this size should provide at least $8 million to help support the restoration programs.

A remarkable series of events occurred during the early stages of shifting financial emphasis from the Rockefellers to other sources. The results have to be listed in the miracle category of fund-raising. Above all we needed a new "star" gift to draw attention to our new development program. It wasn't long coming.

We discovered that Lila and Dewitt Wallace, co-founders of *Reader's Digest*, had quietly, almost secretly, been coming to Colonial Williamsburg for fifty years. In later years, we discovered their interest and accorded them VIP hospitality. They were wonderful people to be with, but for many years we had no active fund-raising program and, hence, had never sought their contribution. They loved Williamsburg, and Mr. Wallace began sending an average of one hundred *Digest* employees a year over a five-year period to see the gardens, greens and buildings of the colonial period.

Wallace's interest began with a telephone call.

"Don," Wallace asked, "do corporations ever make their jets available to send employees to Williamsburg?"

When I answered that this had never happened to my knowledge, he said, "I've been thinking about that possibility."

The employees-to-Williamsburg project got under way soon. Wallace would drop by the desks of *Reader's Digest* employees (usually ladies) and ask, "Have you ever been to Williamsburg?" He would invite eight employees a month to make the trip on a *Reader's Digest* jet. Further, he would go to Westchester Airport on a Thursday to see the group off and give each person $50 "spending money" (all expenses were paid). Spouses and children were not invited. When the group arrived at Patrick Henry International Airport near Williamsburg, two large rental cars were waiting for them on the ramp. Eight single rooms were also reserved in advance at the Williamsburg Lodge. Mary and I would have the *Digest* employees come by our home on the Palace Green for a reception each Saturday afternoon. On Sunday afternoon the jet would return to fly the lucky employees home.

While this very personal liaison was under way another unexpected and most fortunate development occurred. Humelsine received a telephone call one afternoon from the Wallaces' office. The caller reported:

> The Wallaces are in Mexico City taking a lengthy and long-planned vacation. Mrs. Wallace, however, is suffering eye problems induced by Mexican smog. Mr. Wallace has called to ask whether accommodations could be obtained at Colonial Williamsburg. They desperately want to continue their vacation—in clean air.

The Wallaces came and stayed for more than a week. They began each day by sitting in separate rooms in the Moody House, writing postcards to friends. Once we were asked by

Mr. Wallace for 250 postcards, "the ones showing the tulips in the Palace Gardens." He insisted on paying for them. On another occasion we arranged to have a special doorplate printed for the Moody House. It said "Wallace House, not open to the public." They both loved that personal touch and took the plate home with them.

Soon after Thaler arrived in 1976, he sparked an effort to determine whether the Wallaces would be interested in some share of the $13 million plan to advance Colonial Williamsburg's history and heritage programs. After some time, Mr. Wallace replied that he would be interested in a $4 million phase, namely, a new visitor's center theater to show the orientation film, *Williamsburg: The Story of a Patriot*, a depiction of colonial life that the Wallaces always saw during their visits. We also had mentioned the need for a Decorative Arts Museum, a project with a much higher price tag. Then we passed the word that we hoped the Wallaces would become the "star" we needed to let the public know we were serious about fund-raising and attracting a major gift from outside the Rockefeller family.

When Mr. Wallace heard we really wanted $12 million for the Decorative Arts Museum, he took the news quite calmly. Humelsine and I had gone to High Winds, Wallace's New York home, to bid for the $12 million instead of $4 million initially committed.

Upon hearing the larger request, Mr. Wallace didn't gasp. He just turned slowly to Mrs. Wallace and said, "Lila, this is a fairly heavy sum for me to handle at this time; would you be prepared to help me?"

She answered, "No, DeWitt. While I'm very fond of Williamsburg, you know we never share projects." But she added, "We'll talk about it alone, just the two of us."

In any event, Mr. Wallace soon did increase his $4 million commitment to $12 million. In addition, he set up the DeWitt Wallace Fund for Colonial Williamsburg, a separate not-for-profit corporation with six trustees, to which he also made a gift of 250,000 shares of non-voting Reader's Digest Association common stock that was expected to produce an annual income of at least $600,000 for operational support of the DeWitt Wallace Decorative Arts Gallery and Colonial Public Hospital.

By 1990, through a twenty-for-one stock split, the DeWitt Wallace Fund for Colonial Williamsburg owned 5,000,000 shares of *Reader's Digest* stock. In February 1990, this fund joined other Wallace funds (established for the benefit of the Metropolitan Museum of Art, Lincoln Center, Hudson Highlands, Macalester College, New York Zoological Society and Sloan-Kettering Institute) in offering one-quarter of their individual holdings for public issue on the New York Stock Exchange. The sale of the 1,236,681 shares of *Reader's Digest* owned by Colonial Williamsburg brought in $23 million. Further, the remaining 3,763,319 shares in the fund means the total Wallace contribution could reach $100 million or more! This huge total would be eclipsed only by a very few philanthropic gifts ever made to non-profit institutions.

At any rate, the Humelsine-Gonzales visit to the Wallaces had been very profitable for Colonial Williamsburg. Colonial Williamsburg now had the big non-Rockefeller gift it needed. Moreover, the gifts were far larger than we ever dreamed! And the amount increases annually because of the stock income.

Backed by the Wallaces' commitment, the fund-raising pace quickened with the addition of other major gifts by Elizabeth and Miodrag Blagojevich of St. Mary's, Maryland; Mr. and

Mrs. Walter Annenberg of Philadelphia; Abby and George O'Neill of the Rockefeller family and residents of Oyster Bay, New York; Joseph and June Hennage of Chevy Chase, Maryland and Williamsburg; The Winthrop Rockefeller Charitable Trust; and The Rockefeller Brothers Fund. Many other individuals, foundations and trusts also provided valuable furniture, furnishings and major financial resources to augment and strengthen Colonial Williamsburg "That the Future May Learn From the Past."

With such an impressive start, the list of donors to Colonial Williamsburg is now beyond 40,000 — and climbing!

From the start, DeWitt Wallace was a joy to talk with. Sometimes he would call several times a day as he became more and more enthusiastic about the Williamsburg project. At the end of one summer day I wrote to Mary, who was vacationing with our children at Interlochen, Michigan:

> Mr. Wallace called me yesterday for the second time. Always mentions you! A blessed man. I feel he will give Colonial Williamsburg something on the order of $4,000,000. He said as much yesterday, but nothing in writing yet. He has gone up from a new Patriot Theater to adding a craft demonstration center. Oh Boy!

It was "Oh Boy," for sure! I had never participated in raising money before, except for garage, PTA, cookie sales and the like. And here I was starting in the millions. Of course, I understood it was a one-time fluke, and I realized how lucky we were to have professional advice and guidance from Thaler. But even our development expert was not prepared for the sudden go-ahead from Wallace. Thaler said, "Don, you don't raise money that way. You are supposed to go into great research, conceptual drawings, work for a year. You don't raise that kind of money with only a letter and a stamp!" He laughed and noted that the quick response undoubtedly was based on the years of our entertaining the Wallaces and *Reader's Digest* employees. Then he stated what I was coming to learn as a truism about fund-raising: "People Give to People" rather than to causes and institutions. They give to people they know and trust. We, of course, also had another big advantage with Wallace and other donors. We had a great product.

No institution ever had a more enthusiastic donor than Wallace, who became Colonial Williamsburg's number-one promoter. We were always able to reach him on the telephone, to receive quick responses by mail or to make an appointment to see him. With regard to this major gift he wrote:

> It is indeed a privilege for me to make this gift to assist Colonial Williamsburg in preserving our heritage for the future.
>
> I'm confident the stream of public support for this witness to the nation's historic spiritual grandeur will burgeon in future generations. Colonial Williamsburg deserves the support of all Americans as everyone must agree that it is the most significant and fascinating historical restoration in America. Williamsburg is so much a part of our country's history, heritage and patriotic spirit that I wish there was a way everyone could spend at least three or four days in Williamsburg. There is no question that the experience received by young and old alike visiting Colonial Williamsburg is not, and cannot be, equalled anywhere, for Williamsburg's history and heritage are so much a part of our nation's birth.

We also had the quick and responsive support of Wallace's attorney and confidante, Barney McHenry, who followed through on the intricate details of the Wallace gift and made sure it was completed after Wallace's death.

Dedication of the DeWitt Wallace Gallery for the Decorative Arts on June 8, 1985, was a gala occasion. It was the first public acknowledgment that two prominent American families, the Rockefellers and the Wallaces, were working together at Williamsburg. The project underlined the fact that the two families had engaged in many other major philanthropic partnerships, including gifts to the Metropolitan Museum of Art, YWCA, Monet Gardens in Giverny, France, Memorial Sloan-Kettering Cancer Center, New York Public Library and projects in the Hudson River Valley.

Speaking for his family at the dedication ceremonies, Laurance S. Rockefeller told the distinguished audience, including Chief Justice Warren E. Burger:

> As a long-time friend and partner in many projects, I bear witness to the Wallaces' generosity, their interest, their involvement and the fruits of their imaginations. They brought the same action-oriented creativity to philanthropy which they brought to their brilliant publications.
>
> Wally was truly inspired by Williamsburg. In part, he saw reflected here his own concept of the *Digest*'s mission—to keep reminding all of us—now and in the future—of the priceless heritage of our democracy.
>
> What he saw and what he experienced here, of course, was exactly what Father dreamed of in restoring Williamsburg. Wally's beliefs and Father's beliefs tie together in a most extraordinary and mutually-enhancing way.
>
> How pleased Father would have been that Lila and Wally have laid the cornerstone of public financial support for Williamsburg through their enormous generosity.
>
> They have set the precedent in demonstrating the necessity of public assistance for the continued excellence of this national treasure!

Given the opening of the new DeWitt Wallace Gallery and with a new fund-raising program firmly supported by so many American citizens, corporations and foundations, what would John D. Rockefeller, Jr., have thought of such broad private support for the project he bankrolled alone for thirty-three years?

Rockefeller undoubtedly answered the question when he said back in 1941, "It doesn't matter who does a thing. The achievement is what matters. If something is noble and fine, it doesn't make any difference whether the man who did it is Smith or Jones or Brown, if you're lucky enough to be any of them. The doer is not important, either to the public or himself."

Against this sturdy and promising background, Colonial Williamsburg summoned up two additional resources to promote its financial strength. It was obvious that the project was off to an excellent start, but it was equally clear the development framework required a much broader scope.

The first move was the creation of the Raleigh Tavern Society, an organization of substantial donors who were to contribute a minimum of $5,000 annually. David Brinkley, veteran television commentator, long-time advocate of Colonial Williamsburg and a Trustee

DAVID BRINKLEY, A TRUSTEE FOR
TWENTY-FOUR YEARS, STILL HEADS
THE RALEIGH TAVERN SOCIETY,
CW'S GROUP OF LEADING DONORS.
HERE HE LEADS A TOUR OF
EDUCATIONAL PROJECTS.

THE ANTIQUES FORUM HAS BEEN
A BIG DRAW FOR DECADES. AT THE 1949
FORUM, ALICE WINCHESTER AND
MRS. GEORGE M. MORRIS WERE
PHOTOGRAPHED ADMIRING CHINA.

for twenty-four years, became the Society's first chairman. Brinkley's hands-on direction prompted a quick and enormous public response.

Started in 1979, the Raleigh Tavern Society by 1991 had nearly two hundred "big givers" who had already contributed more than $17 million in unrestricted funds to Colonial Williamsburg. Members enjoyed a big dividend by being able to hear Brinkley's first-hand candid and current reports on his views of national and world affairs.

When he retired as a Trustee in 1990 upon reaching seventy years of age, Brinkley voiced his continuing belief in and support for Williamsburg and its stirring history and, at the same time, revealed why he had agreed to chair the Raleigh Tavern Society back in 1979. He also disclosed the most welcome news that he would continue "in retirement" to lead the Society.

With evident emotion, Brinkley recalled how in colonial times the Raleigh Tavern had been the gathering place for the first discussions by George Washington, Thomas Jefferson, Patrick Henry and other early American patriots of their hopes to rid themselves of the British and to create an independent, democratic nation.

"So," said Brinkley, "Williamsburg's Raleigh Tavern is really sort of a holy shrine, in my opinion. Where else in this world did anything like those concepts of individual freedom and democracy unfold—nowhere! Williamsburg is a place that if you really understand what happened here and at the Raleigh it gives you goose bumps!"

A second resource also developed into a worthy arm for Colonial Williamsburg's financial support. It came unexpectedly from the Antiques Forum. Founded in 1949 by Colonial Williamsburg and Alice Winchester, long-time editor of *The Magazine Antiques*, the Antiques Forum had assembled by 1991 a Williamsburg "alumni list" of more than 27,500 Americans interested in the decorative arts. Forum members developed into an enthusiastic and loyal group of supporters who, it seemed sometimes, were seeking a voice in shaping Colonial Williamsburg's progress. Included on the ever-expanding list of registrants were devotees of Williamsburg and the arts who had considerable philanthropic means and important collections of eighteenth-century furniture and furnishings. The "alumni" responded generously when Colonial Williamsburg sounded the call for contributions.

Elizabeth Stillinger, author of the inspiring book, *American Antiques—The Hennage Collection*, stated that the "Williamsburg Antiques Forum has probably had more influence on America's collecting taste and ideas about the past than any other comparable institution."

Wendell Garrett, the erudite and eloquent arbiter of Americana for Sothebys and who succeeded Miss Winchester as editor of *Antiques*, noted in 1990 that forty-three years after its founding, the Williamsburg Antiques Forum "to this day remains unique in its format and unrivaled in its attendance."

In summary, the search for a financial future for Colonial Williamsburg resembled a jig-saw puzzle that was finally falling into place. A good development program must have a good product, and Williamsburg's 300-year-old product could not have been better. It not only championed the work of the founding fathers who forged the democratic principles that guided the future of the young nation, it created a modern-day framework that inspires citizens, foundations and corporations to carry on those principles forged here three centuries ago.

PRESIDENT JOHNSON FOLLOWS
THOMAS JEFFERSON

I can say now that when a President of the United States comes to visit you can count on all hell to break loose. But no one in Colonial Williamsburg in November 1967 could have predicted the chaos of Lyndon Johnson's visit as the weekend guest of the Gridiron Club.

Nothing went as planned. From the moment he arrived by helicopter on the lawn of the Williamsburg Inn, we encountered mind-boggling incidents, unbelievable snafus and disasters that would have made the redoubtable Patrick Henry quail. As the one centered squarely in the eye of the operational storm, I never came closer to spontaneous ulcers or a sudden heart attack as crisis after crisis spread like wildfire.

This was the setting: Washington's most prestigious group of journalists, the Gridiron Club, presided over that year by Walter Trohan, venerable Washington correspondent for the *Chicago Tribune*, decided to hold its first Gridiron roasting outside the nation's capital in half a century. This was a big event. For in addition to Johnson and the journalists, guests were invited from the cabinet, diplomatic corps, Congress, industry and other representatives of America's top ranks. No errors were allowed. Everything had to be perfect. Well, it didn't turn out that way at all! It was soon clear we couldn't control all the forces that were to be unleashed against us.

In a futile attempt to make certain everything went right, Burke Davis, a staff writer, and I were dispatched to Arkansas to brief Winthrop Rockefeller on the fine points of a Gridiron Club evening. First, dress would be white tie and tails. Second, Winthrop would be the host speaker as well as speaker for the Republican Party. Traditionally a Republican and a Democrat tossed only seven or eight minutes of finely honed jests and barbs at each other before devoting a minute or so to semi-serious suggestions of how to work together for the national good. We emphasized to Governor Rockefeller, who was also Colonial Williamsburg's Board Chairman, that ten minutes was all the Republican spokesman and the President of the United States, a Democrat, could have, *period!* We broke up late at night and Davis and I had a first draft by breakfast time. Redrafts were to be sent by mail. We assumed that part of the evening was nailed down and off to a good start.

PRESIDENT AND MRS. JOHNSON GREETED BY THE REVEREND COTESWORTH PINCKNEY LEWIS AS CHARLES ROBB, VIRGINIA'S FUTURE GOVERNOR AND SENATOR, WATCHED.

Hundreds of hours of planning, scores of committee meetings, constant telephoning and any number of trips to Washington were logged, and an elaborate "Operation Plan—Gridiron" was assembled.

The big night arrived and so did Lyndon Johnson and party. My first job was to keep track of Rockefeller and Mills E. Godwin, Governor of Virginia, and move them forward when the White House helicopter landed at the Williamsburg Inn.

Just as we were ready to move to the steps of the helicopter, I suddenly saw a cur-like dog skittering around the legs of the two governors. I thought it was from the neighborhood and would likely bite at least one of the VIPS in the leg. So I began kicking the blasted dog as I tried to connect Rockefeller and Godwin with Johnson. Once I back-heeled the dog in the ribs. It yelped in pain. As the three gentlemen were whisked away by limousine I stayed to watch the helicopter leave. To my utter surprise there sat the errant dog in the helicopter seat just vacated by Johnson! The "cur" was the dog made famous by Lynda Bird Johnson, who had found it weeks before in a parking lot and had taken it to the White House, where it had become a full member of the Johnson family. I suddenly realized with a chill that *I* could have become famous. If I had achieved my earlier wish of nailing the animal with a better kick, I could have killed the dog beloved by the President of the United States! This was only an omen of things to come that fateful weekend.

The white-tie dinner began. Trohan gave his presidential "the Gridiron only singes it never burns" talk "in the dark." The low lights made the Secret Service agents assigned to President Johnson nervous and extra alert. Rockefeller, with his carefully prepared, nine-minute speech, got up and drew a laugh from the audience when he began—"I'm one of five brothers." He read a half dozen more great one-liners, and soon the bigwigs knew Winthrop Rockefeller was a gifted public speaker. With this success in hand, Rockefeller left his text and rambled on and on—about Arkansas, his cattle, life on the mountain, etc. He lasted half an hour!

The next course was to be terrapin soup. It got cold. There were yawns. Winthrop finished off by arching his leg and placing it on the head table to prove he was wearing alligator boots—under his white tie outfit! With that he sat down—at last.

Relieved, we signaled for the terrapin soup, a Gridiron tradition, and the highly trained waiters entered carrying tureens. All went well until a waiter tripped. There was a brief and harmonic crash. Eight tureens of terrapin supreme went through the air, hard and true, straight across the strings of a grand piano and over the keyboard, spilling all the way.

I had never had ulcers. "This must be the night," my stomach told me so. And the evening had hardly started.

Hours later, Johnson got up and delivered one of the evening's better talks. At one point, he referred to his embattled public status because of the Vietnam war. Hostility was so high at that time, he could only visit military bases where his aides and commanding officers could guarantee friendly audiences. Johnson passed off his political plight with this quip, "I understand one of your Williamsburg archaeologists dug up a board the other day. It said—'Dump Jefferson.'"

The night was far from over. At midnight the Gridiron diners were up for more coffee and rounds of liqueurs. A colleague suddenly appeared, obviously upset, and reported, "Don, one of the White House reporters is in jail!" I was incredulous. "You gotta be kidding." Ted Sell of the *Los Angeles Times*, one of the bedraggled bevy of reporters who had covered Johnson's trip to military bases for three days prior to Williamsburg, was smack in the Williamsburg jail. Sell was in a cell! After an encounter with a Williamsburg City policeman, one of scores of police and Secret Service assembled for the occasion, Sell told off the cop. He referred directly to the policeman's ancestry on his mother's side. Bingo, Sell is in the jail. In white tie and tails I hurried to the jail, which was then adjacent to the Lodge parking lot. I could see him through the barred window, writing on a reporter's pad on his knee. I figured the lead of his very exclusive story would be something like, "This is worse than Mississippi!" I also knew such a story would overshadow every good report we had expected from this gala evening.

I found the insulted policeman, discovered he hadn't yet booked the irate journalist and implored him to forget it all. I said, "We are all uptight tonight with the President here. Everyone is thinking of what happened to Kennedy in Dallas. You were doing your job. But your own case shouldn't dominate the news, as it will, if we don't act quickly. Let's try to take his story away from him as best we can." He got the keys to Sell's cell and told him he was free, at last! I escorted the reporter to his bureau chief, Bob Donovan, an old friend, who welcomed the "prisoner exchange."

I finished the night at 4:00 A.M., afraid to face the impending day. But more surprises began soon after daylight.

During advance preparations for the Gridiron weekend, the White House said the Johnsons would plan to attend services at 11:00 A.M. at historic Bruton Parish Church. Humelsine, to make sure the content of the sermon would be appropriate, checked with the minister, the Reverend Cotesworth Pinckney Lewis. He outlined his text as Isaiah 9:2. It sounded fine to Humelsine. But during his sermon, with the President of the United States in the front pew, Lewis interjected—to Humelsine's astonishment—a section on Vietnam and asked the President, "Why?" Of course, there was no answer from Johnson. When the church service ended, reporters flocked to the President and his wife. One asked Mrs. Johnson what she thought of the service. She replied quickly, "Wonderful choir." The news correspondents finally had a story. It had all the ingredients a good story needed in those days, especially a Vietnam angle, and in church! Headlines swept around the world on Monday morning, such as "Minister Attacks Johnson."

Fortunately, I was spared a first-hand encounter at the church. My first job was to be in charge of the motorcade from Bassett Hall, the Rockefeller residence where the Johnsons were staying, to the church. Then I left to go to the golf shop to coordinate a golf game for the President, Representative Jake Pickle of Texas and young Charles Robb, Lynda Bird Johnson's boyfriend at the time.

At the request of the Secret Service, we started the group off on the second tee. We had radio contact between the golf shop and the golfers. The radio came on soon after the golfers teed off.

"Do you have any size thirteen golf shoes?" the voice asked. That meant the President's feet were hurting, what else? We scurried around, found a larger pair of shoes and sent them off by cart and messenger. (Several months later a local golfer asked George Tinsley, the Williamsburg professional, what had happened to the golf shoes worn by the President. "They are over there on that half-price table," George replied casually. For $18 the man bought the "historic" shoes. They were auctioned off later for $500 to charity.)

When I arrived at the Press Room after the game ended I heard what had happened at the church some hours before.

After filing their dispatches on the rector and his sermon, the reporters started an informal competition on Western Union message blanks. The game was to write the most biting sarcasm on the morning's religious service in the most irreligious way.

The White House Press Corps had a field day as reporters posted the fake Western Union messages on a bulletin board in the Williamsburg Lodge Press Room. I went around the room later that night to gather up the best quips on the Reverend Lewis's sermon on Isaiah 9:2. Here are some of them:

Williamsburg, Va.—The Rockefeller Foundation today applied for emergency disaster relief funds.

Acts of God was the reason given for the application.

According to Dr. Cotesworth P. Lewis, rector of Bruton Parish Church in Williamsburg, "Ours is not to do or die, ours is but to question why."

Williamsburg—The White House indignantly denied tonight that President Johnson had placed a Confederate $10-bill in the collection plate at Bruton Parish.

Williamsburg—A White House spokesman says President Johnson has accepted a long-standing invitation from the Bishop of San Antonio and Cardinal Spellman to join the Roman Catholic Church . . .

Attention White House Press:

Washington, November 12, Sunday—A spokesman for the National Council of Churches announced this afternoon that all aid to the Episcopal Church of America has been withdrawn. He also announced that aid to the Church of Christ has been increased, effective immediately.

Washington—President Johnson late today announced the appointment of a high-level, blue-ribbon commission of scholars to study and determine the real meaning of *Isaiah 9:2*. The Commission is to make a special report to him within 30 days.

Williamsburg, Va.—The White House today declined comment on the Rev. Dr. Cotesworth Pinckney Lewis' sermon on Vietnam.

High administration officials, however, called attention to President Johnson's recent speech at McConnell Air Force Base, Kan., in which he praised the Air Force for its skill in "precise pinpoint bombing."

Williamsburg, Va.—President Lyndon B. Johnson attended services here today in historic Bruton Parish Church, which has been in continuous use since 1715. After hearing the rector, the Rev. Dr. Cotesworth P. Lewis, President Johnson appointed him his new spiritual adviser.

BRUTON PARISH CHURCH APPEARS FAR MORE SERENE IN THIS SCENE THAN IT WAS
ON THE DAY OF PRESIDENT JOHNSON'S VISIT IN 1967.

President Johnson said Sunday that the Prophet Isaiah will pay a state visit next month to discuss matters of mutual interest.

Williamsburg, Va.—President Johnson left Williamsburg late Sunday by helicopter. As he boarded, he was singing, "Give me that old-time religion."

The sermon gave the media a chance to joust at the minister's expense and brought out some of their normally hidden literary and reportorial talents.

Later on that evening I heard that Humelsine, furious at the rector's remarks, had vented his anger on the steps of the church while I was off to the Golden Horseshoe Golf Course. Holding back just a bit, he told the assembled media that Lewis's sermon was in "exquisite bad taste." The following day he wrote Johnson that he was "mortified, dumbfounded and dismayed" at the Reverend's "inexcusable and totally inappropriate comments."

Lyndon Johnson, however, rose above the minister's chiding. Several days later he sent Humelsine a message, saying he really bore no ill-will towards the minister at Bruton Parish Church.

I made a copy of Johnson's letter and tossed it in a file. Nearly twenty-two years later, I recovered it and offer it as Johnson's measured rebuttal to the Reverend Lewis.

THE WHITE HOUSE
WASHINGTON

November 15, 1967

Dear Dr. Humelsine:

I am very grateful to you for your letter. Going to Williamsburg is always a pleasure for me; I only wish I could lengthen each visit I make there.

As for the sermon, I have no regrets for having heard it. I know Reverend Lewis was speaking out of a deep concern over the tragic war in Vietnam. I trust he and his congregation grant me the same concern. It may be that I, and those who preceded me in this Office, have made mistakes in regard to American policy towards Vietnam. But they were not, I believe, mistakes of conviction, nor did they proceed from a lack of moral concern. In any event, our visit was as relaxing and rewarding as we had expected it to be. For your courtesy and thoughtfulness to us, please accept our gratitude.

Sincerely,
/s/ Lyndon B. Johnson

Dr. Carlisle H. Humelsine
President
Colonial Williamsburg
Williamsburg, Virginia 23185

An interesting note was appended to the President's letter as follows:

THE WHITE HOUSE
WASHINGTON

Dr Humelsine

The President asked me to tell you that—if you choose or think it desirable—you may show this letter to any member of the congregation or anyone else.

It was a pleasure to see you again.

Warm good wishes, always.
/s/ Juanita Roberts

Juanita Roberts
Personal Secretary
to the President

Humelsine and I never discussed Johnson's letter. We had had enough of the Johnson-Gridiron weekend and, especially, quite enough of the church incident. We had no appetite to stir up the headlines and mixed memories again.

The Reverend's question on Vietnam asked of the defenseless President provided an amazing public reaction. When the story was aired by radio and television and printed in Monday morning's newspapers nearly every comment sided with the President. By Tuesday the mail arriving at the Bruton Parish Church office and at Colonial Williamsburg reflected pro-Lewis positions. The public clearly began siding with the underdog.

At the next regular Gridiron dinner in Washington, the Rector-Johnson incident was recalled in a hilarious skit. Lewis was invited as a very special and now world-famous guest. Also invited was Sonny Jurgensen, quarterback for the Washington Redskins, owned by George Preston Marshall.

"Sonny Jurgensen spoils George Marshall's Sunday afternoons," intoned one Gridiron commentator.

"The Reverend Cotesworth Pinckney Lewis spoils President Johnson's Sunday mornings," added another Gridironer.

The Reverend Lewis, years later, told a writer, "Perhaps some day it will be understood that my remarks were neither derogatory to nor critical of the President. Deplorable misconstructions have been drawn from the occasion by lifting portions out of context, by impugning motives and by imagining ideas which were never stated or inferred."

The incident bubbles up now and then, evading the final "Amen."

The people that walked in darkness have seen a great light:
they that dwell in the land of the shadow of death,
upon them had the light shined.

ISAIAH 9:2

EISENHOWER AND CHURCHILL

Being in the thick of things at Williamsburg for twenty-five years led me into all kinds of VIP experiences from extraordinary to bizarre.

Frequently, I delivered top-level invitations from Winthrop Rockefeller to VIPS to attend a five-star event in Williamsburg. For a most unusual experience on this kind of mission, I drove to Gettysburg, Pennsylvania, to deliver an invitation to Dwight D. Eisenhower. I had a ten-minute appointment with Ike that lasted for two fascinating hours. Although the former President and one-time allied commander had returned to his farm at Gettysburg, the appointment was set for his post-White House office on the campus of Gettysburg College. The complete surprise was the view Ike gave *me* of Williamsburg when he visited there with Sir Winston Churchill soon after World War II.

I rang the doorbell just as I would at anyone's home. An aide to Eisenhower answered; I was identified and admitted. On the first floor a few changes had been made to make the home into an office. But it was quite obvious that some of his aides, who once had occupied fine offices in the White House, were now making do in the living room, study and sun-porch.

After a brief chat, I was taken upstairs to see Eisenhower. His office was in the former master bedroom and it was most attractively decorated. Some of his most prized possessions, including flags, were placed around the room. A few mementoes were in an adjacent area that had been a dressing room.

It was quite a surprise to find the General in these modest surroundings. But this was all forgotten as he got up to shake hands with his usual friendly manner and quick smile.

I told him it was a nostalgic visit for me as I had been one of three reporters who had flashed the word of his decision to run for a second term following his 1956 meeting at Gettysburg College with Senator Knowland. I told him how the three of us wire service reporters (AP, UP and INS) had made a pact at the Administration Building not to use the telephones on the campus as we knew there were only eight circuits out of Gettysburg; that they might be tied up; and, partly guided by the law of self-preservation, how we wanted to

ON THEIR VISIT TO RALEIGH TAVERN, SIR WINSTON AND IKE TOASTED THE MOTTO OF THE ORIGINAL TAVERN: "JOLLITY, THE OFFSPRING OF WISDOM AND GOOD LIVING."

file our stories from our own wires at our downtown Western Union press room. We broke out of the building, each watching the other two like hawks, and all suddenly realized we didn't have any transportation. We had to run about eight blocks. I told him that we intercepted a professor who drove us to the press room, and "that, sir, is the way the world finally found out about your decision." He laughed heartily at this bit of history.

During the chat I asked Eisenhower about his golf game. He reaffirmed his avid interest but noted his scores "could be better." I recalled how Bob Clarke of INS and I once followed him, his golf partners and a squad of Secret Service agents around the Gettysburg golf course. Bored with sitting around the press room at the Gettysburg Hotel, we told Jim Hagerty where we would be that afternoon — playing golf behind the "Eisenhower foursome." Bob and I figured we had it made with our own "work and play vacation," a phrase Hagerty frequently used to describe Ike's absences from the White House.

"Mr. President," I said, "while we were playing behind you, Bob and I decided we would not hit the ball when we were on parallel fairways, lest we loft a ball in your direction. A local player, with no concern at all for your safety came up behind us and asked if he could go through, as we were waiting for you to leave our potential slice zone. We told the golfer it was okay with us but we pointed out, 'Eisenhower is playing just over there. We are afraid we might hit him.'

"'Hell,' he replied, 'he plays here all the time.'"

He then proceeded to tee up and slice a terribly errant shot far to the right toward Ike and even over his head! When the Secret Service agents glared in our direction, we dropped our clubs, held up our innocent hands and pointed to the local culprit. Eisenhower laughed as I recounted the story, saying he remembered the incident and how lucky he was it was a miss.

He seemed so relaxed we just continued chatting, and he recalled his emergency operation for ileitis. He said that was a close call, and that the doctors had decided to operate only after normal bowel functions had been blocked. The operation was successful, and the White House Press Corps moved immediately to Walter Reed Hospital, where we stayed for about ten days. Then the media got the word that Ike was recovered enough to go to his Gettysburg farm to convalesce. What a trip it was!

When White House newsmen cover the President, they are always aware that sudden crises can occur, such as John Kennedy's death in Dallas. They must be constantly alert, especially wire service reporters who have thousands of paying clients around the world depending on them for the first word.

With this responsibility in mind, the three wire services (in those days AP, UP and INS) were gathered at the hospital awaiting Ike and Mamie's motor trip to Gettysburg. When Mamie went on trips she preferred Chrysler limousines. When Ike went alone he preferred Cadillacs.

When the Eisenhowers came out of the hospital and got into her Chrysler it was the first time we had seen the President since his operation. As he appeared, the sun went under a cloud, making Ike look even paler than he really was. But my clear impression was that he was, indeed, a very sick man. He looked awful.

Ike always liked to be in the lead car so he could see better. Therefore, his car was always first with the Secret Service car following. The third car was the wire service car. On orders of the Secret Service all White House motorcade cars were driven in a staggered pattern so no one could pass. Hence, the Eisenhowers' car was to the right, Secret Service car in the left lane, wire service to the right, etc. Although all went well at first, the lead car with the Eisenhowers suddenly veered off to the side of the road near Rockville, Maryland, and came to a dusty halt. We could see only a pillow where Ike was sitting. Our first thoughts were, "He's dead . . . he's had another attack."

My first reaction was to look for telephone wires. There was just one going to an isolated house. I wondered if I could outrun Clarke and Doug Cornell of the AP.

We three nervous competitors jumped out of our car simultaneously to determine how Ike was and why we had stopped. We were told that the liner under one of the rear hub caps had come loose and was hitting the Chrysler's fender, nothing more. An agent pulled the liner loose and off we went, wondering when we would stop again and if Ike would make it. The entourage arrived at the farm without further incident. For my part I always felt the President would have been better off and far more comfortable in an ambulance for that harrowing journey. However, you soon learn at the White House that appearance (for example, the way such a trip is made) figures importantly in times of tension. And Jim Hagerty was a master at the art of Presidential appearance.

When the former President and I completed this reminiscence of a very difficult time for him, I turned the conversation to Williamsburg and the point of my mission. Eisenhower said:

> Well, let me tell you, I really like Williamsburg. I know what it stands for and I believe in it. I just love it. I could get lost there—you know I've been there several times.
>
> In fact, Mount Vernon, Wakefield and Williamsburg are my favorite historical places of that period. Did you ever hear the story of my visit to Williamsburg in March of 1946 with Sir Winston Churchill? Well, I had appeared publicly with him in Washington and I had been embarrassed. The war was just over and everywhere we went the crowds paid too much attention to me.
>
> Anyway we went on to Williamsburg and had a good time. They had some fellows in those colonial uniforms and two or four horses hitched to a barouche. Well, they also had some trumpeters and [showing how] they put the trumpets almost in the ears of the horses and they jumped every which way. Sir Winston didn't pay any attention, he just lit his cigar. I thought, well, those fellows undoubtedly know how to handle horses, or they wouldn't have the job— it wouldn't be right anyway for me to grab the reins. But to be safe I said, "Sir Winston, we had better get out and walk."
>
> He said, "Oh, how far is it? Where are we going?"
>
> I said, "It's just over there—about seventy yards." They wanted us to ride a little ways. Churchill wasn't bothered in the least although I really worried.

At this point, I told him about Colonial Williamsburg's experience with Sir Winston when he was asked whether he would prefer to go to Jamestown or Yorktown. The Prime Minister, in typical fashion, gave everyone the impression he was totally unfamiliar with what the British had suffered at Yorktown.

Mr. Eisenhower laughed, saying, "The British have a great capacity for forgetting unpleasant moments in their history. Once I was talking to three very well-educated Englishmen, from Eton and Oxford, and I started talking about the War of 1812. Well, I got the feeling they didn't know the British had once burned the White House. Oh no, they said they had never heard of that!"

I mentioned a painting on the wall of Ike's office, pointing out that I remembered it as the sycamore tree on his farm from the time I had visited there as a reporter on a tour around the fields and barn. I also recalled seeing his and Mrs. Eisenhower's picture on the cover of the *Saturday Evening Post* and said there was a different tree in the background.

"Yes," he said, "that is the sycamore at the farm. Wyeth did it in two hours, and at the same time he did a little portrait of me about this big (putting his fingers in an oval shape), and that took him about two weeks. He'd put the brush to his lips, twirl it, get it real fine, and then make a tiny dot. He is an excellent artist!"

During our conversation, I had the impression that Eisenhower was really quite lonely and eager to visit. I had expected, based on previous experience, to see him for only a few minutes. But it was understandable that he would want to talk. The setting—a former master bedroom—was a long way from the world's crossroads where he had spent most of his life.

The hour was late when I said how much Winthrop Rockefeller hoped the former President could revisit Williamsburg again. After checking the proposed date on his calendar, he said he would have to regret; maybe some other time.

What an interesting day.

After saying goodbye, I drove to a Howard Johnson's Restaurant on the edge of Gettysburg, bought a cup of coffee and wrote a quick memorandum on this special private interview with Eisenhower. As I drove back to Williamsburg I thought about Ike's visit with Churchill and wondered what had happened behind the scenes while the two men sojourned in the colonial capital fifteen years before. Churchill was always good for colorful sayings and interesting ways of describing various actions, so I made plans to go to the archives. I didn't get back to the job for years, but when I did the predictable rewards were there.

Among other things, I read that Churchill's love for a game of gin rummy had overcome his interest in American history soon after the train reached Williamsburg. After seeing Eisenhower off to Jamestown for the afternoon, John D. Rockefeller 3rd, Churchill and Kenneth Chorley, President of Colonial Williamsburg, found their way back to the Williamsburg depot where the private train was side-tracked.

Rockefeller related this sequence of gambling events:

I was informed they were slipping away for a game of gin rummy, Mr. Churchill being an enthusiastic player having just learned the game on his recent visit to Florida. I decided to join them even though I didn't know the game. For the next hour and a half the three of us sat in the dining room of the private car while Mr. Churchill and Mr. Chorley played. I sat next to Churchill watching his hand. . . . As I became more familiar with the rules, he and I worked together on his hand. . . . While we didn't have a chance to talk the way I would have enjoyed doing with him, there was a friendly give and take during the game that was lots of fun. For example, when he would discard a king he would comment, "Everybody is discarding royalty these days." Then, later a remark was made about his picking up a king and he said, "Somebody has got to stand by the aristocracy."

SIR WINSTON CHURCHILL AND GENERAL DWIGHT EISENHOWER GREETED CHEERING
THRONGS AS THEY RODE DOWN THE DUKE OF GLOUCESTER STREET.

Later, I heard from Duncan M. Cocke, then a rising executive with Colonial Williamsburg, that Churchill started the gin rummy marathon even as the special train left the Richmond station en route to Williamsburg. Cocke heard that Chorley's luck waned to the extent that John D. Rockefeller 3rd, while kibitzing, put his hand on Chorley's shoulder and said, "Don't worry KC, I'll back you up." To that assurance, Churchill was said to have quipped, "If you play gin rummy with me you need a Rockefeller to back you."

Some of the best anecdotal material on the Eisenhower-Churchill visit is discovered in an unpublished memoir by Jean Traverse Chorley. The wife of the President of Colonial Williamsburg recounts her dinner conversation with Eisenhower at the time the two world leaders were visiting in the colonial capital. Mrs. Chorley and Ike were talking about a fateful day in April 1945. General Bradley and Ike had decided to go to the front to visit General Patton. Ike said:

> We arrived there in late afternoon, and spent the evening discussing the war. General Patton never shaved in the morning, but always the last thing at night, so a little while before midnight he said he was going over to his quarters to shave and he turned on the radio for the twelve o'clock news. A little while later we heard someone running outside and General Patton, with

SIR WINSTON CHURCHILL,
ON THE ARM OF KENNETH
CHORLEY, PRESIDENT OF
COLONIAL WILLIAMSBURG,
PARADES WITH GENERAL
DWIGHT EISENHOWER ON
THEIR OFFICIAL VISIT IN 1946.

MRS. CHURCHILL, SIR
WINSTON, MRS. EISENHOWER,
GENERAL EISENHOWER AND
JOHN D. ROCKEFELLER 3RD
(IN THE FRONT ROW) LINE
UP ON THE STEPS OF THE
GOVERNOR'S PALACE.

lather still on one side of his face, dashed into the room. "The President is dead, and they're swearing in the Vice President." Whereupon I said, "Jesus Christ, who *is* the Vice President?"

Ike went on to tell Mrs. Chorley of a talk he had later with President Truman about Washington affairs: "Mr. Truman said to me, 'Ike, get yourself ready for 1948.' I said to him, 'Mr. President, if *you* have no intention of running in 1948, I can tell you now that I don't want any part of 1948 or any other time.'"

To all of this, Mrs. Chorley comments, "I was extremely surprised that General Eisenhower said that to me. I felt I was a complete stranger to him and that he should not have revealed anything like that to me."

Soon after his Williamsburg visit, Churchill went to New York. John D. Rockefeller, Jr., called Churchill at the Waldorf-Astoria Hotel and invited him to dinner. Sir Winston promptly accepted. Then Rockefeller told the brandy-drinking Britisher:

"Mr. Churchill, I think it's only fair to tell you that Mrs. Rockefeller and I do not serve anything to drink in our house."

There was a considerable silence on Churchill's end of the line. Then he said:

"Well, Mr. Rockefeller, won't you and Mrs. Rockefeller have dinner with *me* at the Waldorf?"

Mr. Rockefeller replied quickly, "We'd be delighted."

Churchill's visit to the United States was summed up by him at the conclusion of the dinner given by the Rockefellers, in these Churchillian words:

"Long may Colonial Williamsburg flourish," Churchill intoned. "Firm may be the links which it may forge with our past and may those links of distant by-gone days be reinforced by new links and new bonds which will reach across the ocean and join our two peoples together, which they will have to do."

Sir Winston's long friendship with Williamsburg was noted again at a gala banquet in London given by Colonial Williamsburg's Trustees. Winthrop Rockefeller, as Chairman of Colonial Williamsburg's Board, read a special message from Churchill's old friend, Eisenhower, who said, "In our time, no man has given more to the cause of peace than Sir Winston."

Rockefeller then presented the first Williamsburg Award to Churchill. Its symbol was a hand-crafted silver bell made in Williamsburg. Churchill, in accepting the bell, said:

"Its silver tone is gentle and I shall ring it, I can assure you, whenever I feel there is duty to be done."

These recollections of Churchill bring back my own favorite. During his last official trip to Washington, I joined hundreds of correspondents at a Churchill news conference and luncheon in the ballroom of the Statler Hilton Hotel. After luncheon Churchill answered written questions passed to the head table. The first one chosen was, "Mr. Prime Minister, how would you describe the temperature of Anglo-American relations?"

Churchill got up slowly, black-rimmed glasses pushed as far forward on his nose as they would possibly go. He leaned forward to the microphone, but said nothing. You could have heard a pin drop. He slowly swung his bald head to the right side of the room. Then to the far left side. Then he turned slowly back to the mike, stopped, moved forward and uttered one rumbling and rolling guttural word: "N-O-R-M-A-L." The room exploded in appreciation for what must have been one of Churchill's best answers ever.

JAMES MICHENER, "FRIEND AND WRITER"

Author James Michener and his wife, Mari, were two of Williamsburg's most frequent visitors. Their first visit was initiated by DeWitt Wallace, co-founder of *Reader's Digest*. One morning I was saying goodbye to Wallace at the end of a week's vacation for him and his wife, Lila, at the Williamsburg Inn. Wallace was enthusiastic about their sojourn in the Historic Area, a spring choir concert at The College of William and Mary and visits to nearby Jamestown and Yorktown. He commented, "I have a friend who is a writer—I'd like him to do an article on Williamsburg, but he has suffered a heart attack and may not be up to coming here just yet." After he had talked at considerable length about his "writer friend," I asked his or her identity. Wallace replied, "Oh, he is James Michener." Several days later I wrote Wallace and said we would welcome Michener any time, with great pleasure. Wallace and Michener set an arrival date with the proviso that, first, the visit was to be primarily therapeutic, and, second, he would write about Williamsburg only if he felt like it.

Michener and Mari arrived and vetoed staying at a VIP lodging, the Moody House, because of the stairs to the bedrooms. They chose a ground-floor room near the entrance to the Inn and stayed for a week, moving around Williamsburg, Jamestown and Yorktown as recommended by Wallace. Mary and I enjoyed frequent meetings with the Micheners, including visits at our home and dinner at the Williamsburg Inn and Kings Arms Tavern. Our hopes for a terrific article in *Reader's Digest* on Williamsburg were high. With Wallace and Michener working together how could we miss? But miss we did—after some weeks of vaulting euphoria.

Preceded by lots of hope, the bad news came in a long Michener memorandum to Wallace written from Pipersville, Pennsylvania. Michener mailed a copy to me. It started out O.K. to "Dear Wally" and reported "a fine visit at Williamsburg and I hope that your affairs and mine are in as good condition as theirs seem to be. I think that Carl Humelsine and his colleagues are giving that district a very sensible administration. I liked everything I saw." He then outlined four super story possibilities on the Historic Area. Right on!

On page 2 of the personally typed, single-spaced memo the other shoe dropped. To Wallace, Michener confessed a life-long love and frustration centering on the National Gallery of

DONALD AND MARY GONZALES, SEEN HERE IN THE GARDEN OF THE GOVERNOR'S PALACE, OFTEN ENTERTAINED GUESTS AT THEIR HOME NEXT DOOR, THE ROBERT CARTER HOUSE.

Art in Washington, D.C. His fifth choice for an article (he said he would only do "one of these fine stories for you.") would be the twenty-fifth anniversary of the Gallery. Then— "The idea of a first-rate commemorative essay on the Gallery should be prosecuted."

He went on,

As a matter of fact, I am so attached to this gallery that in 1942 I applied for a job on the curatorial staff but I was properly advised, I think, that to attain such a job three requirements were necessary: (1) It would be best if I had graduated from Harvard College, which I had not; (2) It would be helpful if I had come from a distinguished American family which might give me some financial assistance during the long years of apprenticeship, and again I did not qualify; (3) It would be especially useful if I spoke French and German and had married a girl whose parents might be able to help also in my sustenance during the long years of small payment. Three pitches, three strikes and I was out? In my disappointment I turned to writing.

In our "disappointment" we turned to the wailing wall. The die was obviously cast against us. Later that year the *Reader's Digest* proudly featured a birthday article on the "National Gallery of Art by James A. Michener;" nothing on our colonial domain. Nevertheless, the Micheners returned to Williamsburg many times, as Michener had forecast. In his memo to Wallace, he had written, "I had a great stay at Williamsburg for the people there are both knowledgeable and charming, and I know I will be returning to see them in one capacity or another."

During one of his ensuing visits with Mari, Michener established Williamsburg as one of several headquarters for researching *Chesapeake*, and we invited the Micheners to come by the Robert Carter House on the Palace Green, where we lived. We introduced them to the stately house, dating back to 1746. I sensed that this survivor of colonial days and its lore would appeal to the Micheners. We had a framed copy of a page from Washington's diary (the original is now in the Library of Congress) on the wall of our study. The entry, in Washington's handwriting and entitled "Where & How—my time is—Spent," reported the following on November 6, 1769: "Came to Williamsburg. Dind at Mr. Carters with Lord Botetourt Govr. Eden & ca. and suppd at Mrs. Vobes with Colo. Fitzhugh."

We sat on the back porch overlooking the large yard and a far-spreading hackberry tree at least 225 years old, one of the oldest and largest of its kind in the United States. Protected by many lightning rods and other metal supports, the giant tree was fed in the spring by special booster foods poured into holes drilled deep into the ground near its massive roots. (Sadly, a storm felled the great tree in 1989, leaving a stump forty feet around at ground level.)

As we chatted, I told Michener that to my surprise I had found a copy of one of his early books, one I had not known about, while I was prowling around in Arnold's Book Store in Traverse City, Michigan. The title was *Sports in America*. In the book Michener wrote that he had never been able to figure out whether the football capital of the United States "was in Alabama or Nebraska." Knowing that Mary and I were native Nebraska cornhuskers, Michener autographed the book, "To Mary and Don Gonzales, who know where the football capital of America is! /s/ James Michener."

That evening the Micheners, with Audrey and Ivor Noël Hume, Colonial Williamsburg's talented archaeological team, joined us for dinner at the Williamsburg Inn. My wife was seated next to Michener, and during the evening he talked with her about worthy pursuits friends of his had taken up in their retirement years. One name escaped him, and a week or so later Mary received this personal letter from Michener dated April 23, 1977.

Dear Mary,

    The other night at dinner you made an observation to which I did not respond because of other conversation. Through the years I have developed these generalizations:

    A. Men should retire from positions of institutional management—college presidents, automobile manufacturers, heads of police departments, coaches of football teams—even earlier than they do now. Such positions should be in the hands of younger men.

    B. However, when a man has built up a vested financial interest in an organization, he should insist upon remaining on the payroll as long as decently possible, in some lesser capacity if necessary. This preserves his self-respect, his longevity and his income.

    The operative case was that of Outerbridge Horsey, one of the best State Department types I've known. After serving in many secondary positions he finally made ambassador to Roumania, perhaps. At the end of a good term he was told that he must retire, and he said he didn't want to. "All right, you're assistant-consul to Palermo." I'm told that Palermo never had a better or more appreciated assistant-consul.

Our love,
/s/ Jim Michener

During their next visit we mentioned our appreciation for the personal note. This brought up the subject of a Library of Congress project we had never heard about, but which Michener had participated in for many years. The Library of Congress, he said, serves as a permanent repository for literary and personal papers of significant American authors; and he started the flow of copies of his writings to the Library of Congress Manuscript Division in 1949. Control ranges from no restrictions at all for researchers with a valid interest to no access to some financial and legal papers that cannot be seen until the author's death, and still others that cannot be seen until twenty-five years after his death.

Our paths crossed again in the fall of 1986 when we joined the Micheners and The Society of American Travel Writers on a trans-Atlantic crossing on Cunard's *QE II* from New York to Southampton. As a guest lecturer on the trip, Michener spent most of one morning answering questions about his life and writing styles. He told how he prefers to arise early in the morning to write and research until mid-afternoon, and how he visits all areas several times over a period of years before he starts to write. At that time, he had just completed *Alaska* and was heading to the Caribbean for his next book.

Long known as having strong personal ties to the Democratic Party, Michener was asked how he came to prefer the Democrats.

"Well," he replied, "when I was young and living in Doylestown in Pennsylvania, I asked the lady who was raising me, 'What is a Democrat?'

"'Oh,' she replied with obvious disdain, 'they're the kind of people who live down by the railroad tracks, and don't amount to much.'

"I decided then and there I would be one of them."

Is it possible Michener chose that political path because his non-Harvard, undistinguished family background once caused him to be spurned by the National Gallery of Art?

ROMANCING NORMAN ROCKWELL

Colonial Williamsburg, as an educational, not-for-profit institution, always had difficulty promoting its historical appeal through advertising. Working within low budgets, we found it difficult to compete with hotels, cruise lines, resorts and other travel attractions that could afford slick advertising. As a result, we had to rely heavily on publicity from visits of heads of state and major special events commemorated in Williamsburg, like historical anniversaries. At the same time, we knew that advertising had important recall value for radio listeners and newspaper and magazine readers.

The search for a nook or cranny in this over-blown travel marketplace finally resulted in a bonanza Colonial Williamsburg administrators would never have come up with in their wildest dreams.

To get the most bang for our limited funds, Colonial Williamsburg for years employed a New York advertising agency. The distance created a communication problem, and at our infrequent meetings in Virginia we would explain what we wanted and they would tell us what we should do. Neither side was confident the other had the solution. This uneasy, groping relationship was fragile at best.

Finally, in the late 1960s, we broke with the New York group and contracted with a new agency in nearby Richmond, Martin and Woltz, headed by David N. Martin and George Woltz. It was the agency that later coined the endearing "Virginia is for lovers" campaign for the Commonwealth of Virginia. President Humelsine, Tom McCaskey, Rudolph Bares, George Wright and I charged the agency to tell America's traveling public that several historic buildings were opening to the public in the summer of 1968. This was a very important time for us as the attractions were the Wren Building at The College of William and Mary, the Peyton Randolph House on Market Square, the James Geddy Silver Shop and Wetherburn's Tavern. With the related Geddy House, these buildings represented a valuable core of the eighty-eight original Williamsburg structures dating from colonial times. Of cardinal interest, too, was the fact that General George Washington, General Lafayette and General Rochambeau all had stayed in the immediate neighborhood of the

IN A "ONCE UPON A TOWN" TOUR, A GROUP OF VISITING CHILDREN PLAYS GAMES FROM COLONIAL DAYS WITH A COSTUMED DIRECTOR.

CHILDREN ARE TREATED ROYALLY AT COLONIAL WILLIAMSBURG. THIS GROUP IS BEING
TAKEN ON AN OX CART RIDE IN THE HISTORIC AREA.

Market Square during the closing days of the American Revolution at nearby Yorktown.

The task of introducing these historic buildings to the public was a formidable one. We had sufficient historical data on the group, but because the buildings were not yet fully restored, no photos were available for advertising purposes. Deadlines were pressing on us. So also was the question of "taste." At that time, marketing and advertising techniques were suspect in our Williamsburg community, and our far-flung constituency of antiquarians favored keeping the community "pure and quiet," protected from "smelly, noisy buses" and ordinary sightseers. They felt the Historic Area was a precious gem to be kept for connoisseurs only.

Hence, we were starting at zero when we turned the challenge over to Martin and Woltz. In a matter of only a few days, however, the agency came up with an improbable but fascinating suggestion. During her research a young agency staff member, Libby Meggs, discovered pencil sketches Norman Rockwell did during a visit to France. Her idea was to get this world-famous artist to work for the Colonial Williamsburg campaign. Our reaction was "Okay sure, get Rockwell, America's top artist-illustrator for advertising! You must be daft. And for how much? We have budgeted only $250 for each illustration of four buildings! How about being serious?"

What happened? Dave Martin recounts the ensuing events in his book, *Romancing the Brand — The Power of Advertising and How to Use It* (Amacon Books, American Management Association, New York).

Martin picked up the telephone, asked for information in Stockbridge, Massachusetts, got Rockwell's listed number, dialed it and reached the artist on the first ring. Following his brief proposal for Rockwell to sketch the buildings, Martin was told, "I'm working on an illustration of astronauts. Lots of heads. Takes lots of time." Martin sensed Rockwell was indifferent and weary and suggested the artist and his wife might like a vacation, "Williamsburg is a great place to take a vacation."

This hit home. It was winter. "It's awfully cold here in Stockbridge," Rockwell mused. "Do you have snow?"

When Martin expressed shock at such a wintry thought, Rockwell said, "Let me talk with Molly." When Martin called back Rockwell already had made air reservations to arrive the next Sunday in Richmond!

"Molly says it's so cold here, so we're coming to Williamstown," Rockwell said. (He never did get Williamsburg straight as a name.)

With great concern, Martin interjected, "We haven't talked about your fee."

"How much have you got?" the artist asked.

Martin said Colonial Williamsburg's advertising budget for the entire year for radio (no television), newspapers, magazines and other expenses "is only $200,000."

Rockwell laughed, "That's enough. We'll see you at the airport."

One of history's greatest advertising coups was in the making. The "romance" was under way.

Upon arrival at the Richmond Airport, the Rockwells were escorted to Williamsburg by Martin and Woltz, the agency's top executives. As they drove past one of the targets, the Peyton Randolph House, Rockwell reacted immediately! "My, there are a lot of windows. I

This is the Peyton Randolph House. You remember Peyton Randolph, don't you?

200 years ago, he was one of our most influential leaders. Today, he is one of the least remembered.

He was President of the First Continental Congress, Speaker of Virginia's House of Burgesses, Attorney General of the Colony.

In fact, Peyton Randolph presided over nearly every important legislative body in Virginia during the years just prior to the Revolution.

He was also featured on the "most wanted" list of the British.

In 1775, the militia paid him a tribute calling him Father of Our Country. (He died shortly after that and the title went later to his friend George Washington.)

But he left behind a handsome two-story house of warm paneling, marble mantles and heavy walnut doors.

Today this is one of Williamsburg's most distinguished original houses.

Beginning July 1, it will be one of four historic buildings to be added to the Colonial Williamsburg exhibition program.

Come and see the surroundings where one of our early leaders lived and worked.

And you'll always remember him.

COLONIAL
Williamsburg
VIRGINIA

ILLUSTRATOR NORMAN ROCKWELL, ENTHRALLED BY WILLIAMSBURG, DREW FOUR REMARKABLE ADS.

hate to draw windows!" Despite the initial coolness, however, warm temperatures won out and by Tuesday Rockwell had a sketch of Peyton Randolph, curly peruke and all. But where *was* the house? The raison d'être for the proposed ad? Rockwell's drawing showed only the corners of the house poking out behind each end of a broad crape myrtle tree growing above Randolph's peruke head! George Wright took a look and murmured, "He damn well took care of the windows!" There *were* no windows.

Rockwell defended himself, saying, "If you want an accurate drawing of the house, you can engage an architect. But if you want the drawing to help tell a story, then I will do that for you. By adding the portrait (of Randolph) I'm helping you tell the story about the person who lived there."

Rockwell was right, of course. But the word got back to me that there still was trouble with our new-found friend. The grapevine reported that Mrs. Rockwell, as part of her tour, rapped on the door of a privately occupied home in the Historic Area and was promptly invited in for afternoon tea. During teatime repartee, Molly told her hostess who her husband was and mentioned the difficulties he was having pleasing the advertising agency. As soon as my informant called me with the "news," I called Martin in Richmond.

"I hear you are giving Rockwell a hard time — I hear you don't want pictures of people in ads," I reported.

When Martin said he had relented, I said "That's good. Tom (McCaskey) and I have talked it over. If he wants to put people in, let him do it."

Martin was astonished at my knowledge of what was going on, and asked how I knew so much. "Williamsburg is a small town," I replied.

To sum up, Rockwell did all four ads in his own style. They were outstanding illustrations featuring the Geddy Silversmith Shop, Wetherburn's Tavern, the Wren Building and, of course, the long Peyton Randolph House — with a few discernible windows and fewer tree limbs.

The results were phenomenal. As soon as the ads were released, our telephones began ringing at a fantastic rate. People were fascinated with the illustrations and wanted to come to Williamsburg.

What did the Rockwell ads cost? Almost nothing. On the last day of the Rockwells' visit to Williamsburg, Martin popped the question of fees again and apprehensively waited for the master-artist to reply. After a moment Rockwell said, "I'm making so much with the Famous Artists' School, most of what you would pay me would go for taxes anyway. I don't need the money. But Molly and I did need to get away from the cold. If you want, you can take care of our expenses. That will do just fine."

How much should the illustrations have cost? The nearest guess begins with a young waiter at Christiana Campbell's Tavern, located just behind the Capitol in the Historic Area. He asked Rockwell for an autograph. He received a sketch of a little white dog with black spots on the back of a tavern menu with the autograph. Years later, Martin saw the same sketch framed and hanging on the wall of a Rockwell souvenir shop in Vermont. The shop-keeper had purchased it for $2,500! So it seems Rockwell gave the waiter a nifty tip "in kind."

Our best guess is that the four Rockwell illustrations made for "expenses only" had a market value at the time of around $40,000.

VIP PARADE

After Rockefeller and Goodwin reached agreement on restoring Williamsburg, the old capital slowly began drawing worldwide attention. Beginning in the late 1920s and early 1930s, top government officials from abroad—kings, queens, princes and princesses, presidents, prime ministers and their top aides—came in droves. Early visitors were presidents Franklin D. Roosevelt, Harry S. Truman and Dwight D. Eisenhower.

In 1934 President Roosevelt became the first United States VIP to visit Williamsburg. He called the reopened Duke of Gloucester Street "the most historic mile in all America," and, thereafter, the reputation of Williamsburg and its renaissance spread far and wide. In addition, a new wave of top-level visitors came to Williamsburg soon after Humelsine arrived in the 1950s. Drawing on his State Department background, Humelsine teamed up with a former diplomatic colleague, Clement E. Conger, Deputy Chief of Protocol, to entertain more than a hundred chiefs of state in Williamsburg. The normal welcoming procedure was to give VIPS a quiet colonial night to rest up after overseas flights and the next morning to provide a horse and carriage ride before their whirlwind takeoff in a helicopter that flew them directly to the White House.

For twenty-five years we worked with the White House, State Department and scores of embassies in Washington, D.C., trying our very best to welcome global notables while avoiding major faux pas. Operations were planned to the minutest detail by Ran Ruffin, Dick Sessoms, Norm Beatty, Trudy Moyles, Kathy Pickering and many others. Humelsine always screened the finished plan, which could run to sixty pages or more. Despite the careful process, we never could anticipate exactly what would happen and what could go amiss during these visits. Each visit to Williamsburg was different. We could usually count on a lot of surprises and now and then some good laughs. The gamut of threats ranged from assassination attempts and alleged poisoning of foreign leaders to riots and hostile demonstrations. Of course, there were times we felt good about events and how we handled crises that erupted without warning.

Our record as hosts of Colonial Williamsburg is peppered with notable challenges. Trying

PRESIDENT ROOSEVELT CALLED THE DISTANCE BETWEEN THE CAPITOL AND THE WREN
BUILDING, COLLEGE OF WILLIAM AND MARY, "THE MOST HISTORIC MILE IN AMERICA."

PRESIDENT HARRY S. TRUMAN MADE
A FORMAL BUT JOLLY DESCENT
THROUGH COLUMNS OF GUIDES AND
HOSTESSES WHEN HE VISITED THE
GOVERNOR'S PALACE IN 1948.

WHEN ELEANOR ROOSEVELT VISITED
WILLIAMSBURG, SHE CAME WITH HER
GRANDDAUGHTER UNANNOUNCED —
BUT NOT UNRECOGNIZED
BY AN ALERT CAMERAMAN.

PRESIDENT RICHARD NIXON STUDIED
THE LABORATORY OF WILLIAMSBURG
ARCHAEOLOGIST NOËL HUME,
AND MRS. NIXON CHATTED AMIABLY
WITH CURATORS.

PRESIDENT GERALD FORD EXTENDS
A WARM HANDSHAKE TO ONE OF
SEVERAL COLONIAL WILLIAMSBURG
HOSTESSES WAITING IN LINE
TO RECIPROCATE.

PRESIDENT JIMMY CARTER, DRESSED
DOWN IN SPORTS SHIRT AND
SWEATER, ENJOYED A RELAXING
STROLL AROUND THE HISTORIC
SIGHTS IN WILLIAMSBURG.

PRESIDENT AND MRS. RONALD REAGAN
RECEIVED A FIFE AND DRUM SENDOFF
AT THEIR DEPARTURE FROM THE
INTERNATIONAL SUMMIT MEETING IN
WILLIAMSBURG IN 1983.

to keep up with modern celebrities elevated one's colonial blood pressure. The lighter moments snap back most easily in memory, and it's interesting though not surprising to note that more of these happened in the company of Americans than foreigners.

I remember vividly when Shirley Temple, the child movie star turned diplomat, gave me a big surprise. The pert and pretty little lady had first visited Williamsburg in 1938 when she was already famous, and we were pleased when she returned in 1976 for two more visits as U.S. Chief of Protocol, accompanying foreign visitors. On one of the 1976 occasions, we planned a dinner at Carter's Grove Plantation, the splendid estate eight miles from Williamsburg, with a wide vista across the James River.

My first job of the evening was to stop by the cottage where Ambassador Shirley Temple Black was lodged and to take her to Carter's Grove. I arrived on time and knocked on the door. She opened it very quickly. I soon knew why. The rear zipper in her black evening dress was jammed, and she'd been alone with no one to help her.

"Don, would you zip me up?" the Ambassador asked.

What was I to do?

So for my country and its Chief of Protocol, I bravely jimmied the zipper all the way to the top—from the very bottom!

GEORGE BUSH, THEN VICE PRESIDENT, WELCOMED FRENCH PRESIDENT MITTERAND
TO THE YORKTOWN BICENTENNIAL CELEBRATION IN 1981.

SHIRLEY TEMPLE, ALREADY WORLD
FAMOUS AS A CHILD MOVIE STAR,
MADE HER FIRST VISIT TO COLONIAL
WILLIAMSBURG WITH HER
FATHER IN 1938.

AMBASSADOR SHIRLEY TEMPLE BLACK
MADE HER FIRST FORMAL TRIP TO
WILLIAMSBURG AS U.S. CHIEF OF
PROTOCOL TO WELCOME PRESIDENT
KEKKONEN OF FINLAND.

How many people can say they performed that task in the line of duty?

The day before the Carter's Grove dinner and because of a series of unexpected developments, I had spent eight hours with the former child movie star. This was her first formal trip in her new role as the first woman Chief of Protocol in U.S. history. Her mission was to greet Dr. Urho Kekkonen, President of Finland.

To start that ultra-busy day, I met Mrs. Black at Patrick Henry Airport and accompanied her to Williamsburg. At 5:00 P.M., we returned to the same airport for the 6:00 P.M. arrival of the Finnish president. His plane was late, so the Chief of Protocol and I talked about diplomacy, her new job, life in Washington, D.C., her first ambassadorial post in Ghana, her earlier assignment as special U.S. representative to the United Nations and so on. She was charming, gracious, bright, warm and extremely interesting. We talked in a private area away from the autograph seekers who always followed her.

After Kekkonen arrived, he, Ambassador Black and I rode back to Williamsburg in a limousine. He was obviously delighted with his lady hostess with the sparkling eyes, and he chatted about his side trip to Hancock, Michigan, which he described as "like Finland, lots of lakes."

After delivering the President to his VIP quarters for the night, the Ambassador, Mark Evans, a friend of mine from my Washington days, and now U.S. Ambassador to Finland, and I had a leisurely dinner at the Williamsburg Inn to make plans for the next day.

The tour of the Historic Area with the official party turned out to be embarrassing as tourists recognized our ambassador and kept yelling "Shirley Temple . . . there she is," time and time again. The happy observers showed no interest at all in VIP Kekkonen.

During this visit, Fannie Lou Stryker, a veteran hostess for Colonial Williamsburg and wife of Williamsburg Mayor Henry M. ("Polly") Stryker, met Ambassador Black for the second time. She had escorted little Miss Temple during her first visit to Williamsburg thirty-eight years before. On this occasion, Mrs. Black chuckled to Mrs. Stryker, "I finally got as tall as you!"

Another very special VIP visitor was Walt Disney, the inventor and boss of Mickey Mouse, who came to Williamsburg several times to ponder the past and his future creations. Although he liked our low-key historical presentation, Disney had real trouble understanding how a non-profit institution operated financially. One evening at dinner at Kings Arms Tavern he asked me, "How much do those carriages cost, how many do you have, and how much do you charge riders?" I told him we usually ran two or three carriages or wagons with horses; they cost from $8,000 to $10,000 each; one fancy carriage cost approximately $35,000—and all were handmade. As for the price per ride, I told him we were charging $2 per person.

Disney looked at me in total disbelief. Then quickly he solved the problem in his imaginative, profit-making way:

What you should do is mass produce wagons. Put a lot of seats in each one, charge each person twenty-five cents, and keep them going early and late up and down the Duke of Gloucester Street. You'd make a lot of money.

I made a weak response, thinking of the havoc scores of horses would wreak. Pedestrians wouldn't want to walk—probably couldn't walk at all—on our historic streets.

WALT DISNEY, THE WORLD-RENOWNED CARTOONIST, RETURNED TO WILLIAMSBURG SEVERAL TIMES. HERE, IN 1948, HE HAD BEEN CONFERRING WITH STAFF MEMBERS.

When Disney learned some years later that he had terminal cancer, he came back to Williamsburg for a last visit. He sat many hours in the block-long business section near The College of William and Mary. He was never alone. People by the scores recognized him quickly. While chatting with a group of radio students, he confided, "I don't want it publicized that I am going back to the West Coast to go into the hospital." Some of his last days were spent pleasantly holding court outside the Williamsburg Theatre—a final home away from home for him.

One of the specters we always lived with as "State Department South" was the possibility that a diplomatic incident harmful to U.S. relations with foreign countries would occur while chiefs of state or other VIPS were on our colonial turf. The closest we ever came to having the diplomatic apple cart upset in a major way was during the visit of His Majesty King Mohammed V of Morocco.

President Humelsine himself was in the center of the incident that convinced the visiting king he had been "poisoned," no less, in one of *our* taverns. Always the perfect diplomatic host, Humelsine had offered a luncheon for the King and his party at Christiana Campbell's Tavern, one of George Washington's favorite colonial eateries, and the King accepted. In retrospect, perhaps we should have anticipated that something devastating to the equanimity of the King's brief sojourn en route to the White House was likely to occur. For the night before the luncheon, members of the all-male Moroccan entourage refused to leave the King's suite at the Williamsburg Inn. They slept all over the floors in the sitting room and the royal bedroom. They ran up and down the halls of the sedate five-star inn. One aide placed a handmade silver bowl, presented just hours before to honor the King, on his own head, trying to balance it as he darted up and down the corridor.

At any rate, Humelsine's luncheon began quietly. Because the King of Morocco did not drink alcohol he was served a large glass of orange juice. The tavern table was set as it would have been in the eighteenth century with sugar in a pewter shaker and salt in an open bowl with a small spoon—i.e., just the reverse of the setting normally used today. While Humelsine's attention was diverted, the King picked up a large soup spoon, plunged it into the salt (thinking it was sugar) and dumped it into his juice. He picked up the glass and downed a huge swallow. All hell broke loose. The King jumped up, yelling, "I've been poisoned . . . I've been poisoned!" The royal guards and Secret Service assumed the King knew what he was yelling about. Several pistols were quickly in hand. Pandemonium reigned in the small tavern as the King spat out the "poison." Humelsine quickly figured out what had happened and, through an interpreter, explained about the salt. The King was not convinced. His throat knew he had been poisoned, *period!* Finally, after threatening to leave the tavern (if not Williamsburg), his Royal Highness settled down a bit and agreed to go through with the luncheon. However, he appeared furtive, probably suspecting to the end of his visit that his American host was really not to be trusted.

As the list of foreign visitors lengthened, Colonial Williamsburg had to become more and more security conscious. The Allen-Byrd House, usually used as the number-one VIP house, had iron plates across the windows in the master bedroom when President Reagan stayed there. The basement was filled with all manner of surveillance and emergency equipment installed by the Secret Service, army intelligence and other federal experts. Virginia state police, local police, bomb squad specialists and other security personnel were there too.

The most concentrated security measures we ever saw surrounded the visit of Their Majesties, Emperor Hirohito and Empress Nagako of Japan. Long before the royal couple arrived, the Secret Service received a report that Japanese Red Army terrorists planned to assassinate the Emperor—in Williamsburg! As a result, when the Hirohitos arrived, the old city bristled with security, seen and unseen.

One of the most vulnerable moments of the royal visit requiring extra security was the traditional Williamsburg carriage ride. We didn't know whether this activity would occur or not. During official visits, all primary security arrangements were handled by the United States and the foreign government involved, in this case, Japan. In the spirit of tradition, both sides agreed to prepare for a carriage ride down the Duke of Gloucester Street, a pattern set on a previous visit by Queen Elizabeth and Prince Philip. The Japanese aides knew the Emperor wanted the same treatment the British royalty received, and they insisted on securing for their monarch the Queen's Suite, the same one used by the British.

The first major security step required was stripping down the interior of Williamsburg's finest carriage and lining it with steel plates to protect its occupants from gunfire and bombs—

as much as possible. This wasn't easy. The carriage had been handmade and crafted to sustain most kinds of wear and tear. Nevertheless the job was accomplished, and in great haste.

Next, security agencies ordered all second-floor areas of taverns, shops and homes along the carriage route to be evacuated before and during the event. No precautions this rigid had ever been enforced in Williamsburg before (nor have they been since).

The top of the carriage was to be left down, thus making the royal pair indiscernible to the crowd. The Emperor and Empress were so short that they already were well positioned down inside the metal shell created for their basic protection. Security experts assumed positions on the second floor of most buildings to minimize chances of pot shots from above. Finally, at the appointed time, the elegant but armored carriage rocked away from the Williamsburg Inn. Only the top of the royal heads could be seen, minuscule targets for any sharp shooters. Now and then onlookers could see the Emperor's arm waving to them. At any rate the hazardous ride went off without any trouble.

THE EMPEROR AND EMPRESS OF JAPAN ON TOUR WERE BARELY VISIBLE OVER THE RIM OF THE CARRIAGE BUT CAREFULLY PROTECTED BY THE SECRET SERVICE.

One incident helped ease the tension that day. When the carriage reached the Duke of Gloucester's "business" district, it encountered protesters objecting to Japan's killing of whales. Not understanding any of the words on the placards, the Emperor and Empress accepted the demonstrations against them as yet another symbol of America's warm welcome. They applauded the marchers and waved! Confused too, the demonstrators waved back!

Always an exceedingly busy time in the Historic Area, Easter of 1959 was no exception. Indeed, all of Colonial Williamsburg's rooms and restaurants had been booked for weeks before that Easter when a call came from the State Department. The request was for appropriate accommodations, a carriage ride, a special dinner—the complete VIP treatment for King Hussein of Jordan and his party of thirty. To make matters more tense, we knew that David Rockefeller and his family were coming at the same time!

But, we never said no to Washington. We began telephoning people who had reserved the best suites and rooms in the Williamsburg Inn and in nearby colonial houses. There were some reluctant relinquishers but most felt it preferable to defer to a king than to a lesser mortal. Anyway, we worked it out.

Two carriages were required on Easter morning—one for the King and one for the Rockefellers. All went well until the King's carriage plus assorted limousines passed Wetherburn's Tavern, a property on the Duke of Gloucester Street that was still privately owned. The carriage with David Rockefeller and his family was moving toward King Hussein's entourage. As they met, the occupants of each carriage waved. Then, to my utter horror—and that of my colleagues—we saw a labeled dummy hanging by rope from the sign at Wetherburn's Tavern. We could not believe our eyes! The sign on the gently swinging "body" read, of all things, "John D. Rockefeller, Jr."

David Rockefeller was as surprised and shocked, perhaps more so, than anybody. As photographers and reporters flocked to the bizarre scene, Rockefeller asked the driver to stop and dismounted from his carriage to get a better view of his "father" who, for all his Herculean efforts on behalf of Williamsburg, was being hanged in effigy. I left the King's party, as it went on, to walk behind Rockefeller, who went directly into the tavern to get to the bottom of the problem, whatever it was. No one could guess what had triggered such an incident at such a bad, unfortunate time.

What we heard first hand was this: The proprietors of the tavern had been blackballed by the Williamsburg–James City County Chamber of Commerce. The group's hospitality committee decided that the tavern did not meet room, restroom and other sanitary standards. David Rockefeller, after going deeper into the tavern, emerged saying he agreed with the Chamber of Commerce! No one, including Rockefeller, could figure why Williamsburg's deceased benefactor was the target of the tavern management's ire. But, as an Easter attraction, the ploy worked! Publicity exploded from the newspapers, the radio and television. Easter and King Hussein were eclipsed in the media coverage. It took Colonial Williamsburg many moons to recover from the weird and unpredictable events of that day.

We had another major surprise and some tense moments during the final hours of planning for the May 1971 visit of His Majesty King Faisal of Saudi Arabia.

The King was due in Williamsburg by helicopter at 5:00 P.M. Plans were to be completed during my luncheon at noon with the Saudi Arabian ambassador and State Department officials. During our meeting at the Allen-Byrd House, the Inn operator called for the Ambassador to take an urgent message from the King, who had just arrived in Paris.

The King reported that he was stopped in Paris and that he wanted President Johnson to send his personal plane there to pick him up for the final leg of the trip to the United States. After some hasty checking with the White House, we learned that Johnson refused, pointing out it was the King's responsibility to get to Williamsburg and that a White House helicopter would bring him from there to Washington, but nothing more!

The Ambassador relayed the bad news to his King, who was furious at being spurned by his American host. After further fuming, the King relented and chartered a TWA plane for his flight to the United States.

What was Williamsburg to do? The King was arriving seven hours late, so 5:00 P.M. was now advanced to midnight. How could a helicopter from Langley Field land at that hour on the Williamsburg Inn lawn? Williamsburg and government security and fire officials held a hurried meeting. They decided to place huge floodlights on the Inn lawn along with all available emergency equipment. The Inn "heliport" suddenly took on the look of a flashy county fair.

Just after midnight, the helicopter whirred over the Inn's tennis courts and landed the King and his party safely alongside the big white lights. For those of us who had experienced the many behind-the-scenes crises since lunchtime, it was easy to understand why His Royal Majesty was tired and very upset. But for all we could tell the Johnson-Faisal talks in Washington had gone well—on the surface!

Their Majesties King Bhumibol and Queen Sirikit of Thailand were the nicest, most natural visitors we ever had in Williamsburg. They wanted to be treated as ordinary visitors, and they were very curious about the United States and the one-time capital of the eighteenth-century Virginia colony.

Winthrop Rockefeller flew from Arkansas to greet the King and Queen upon their arrival at Langley Air Force Base, about thirty-five minutes from Williamsburg. During the motorcade trip from the airport, the King asked Rockefeller, "What are some Virginia customs?" The Governor of Arkansas wasn't too sure of a quick answer. Then an idea struck him. He replied, "mint juleps," and explained how Virginia natives blend bourbon, ice, sugar and crushed mint leaves. It sounded good to the King. He asked if the royal party could sample "this old Virginia custom," perhaps on the following day, which happened to be July 4. The hour was set for 11:00 A.M. at the Humelsines' home on the Market Square. During the night a search was conducted for silver goblets and pewter tumblers that were promptly put on ice to be frosted.

By 11:00 A.M. the Thai party was sipping its way to an early Fourth of July climax with the sweet-tasting, frosty and flavorful but potent drinks. The conversation pepped up a lot. At one point I crossed over the Humelsines' living room toward the Queen's lady-in-waiting and noticed that her silver tumbler was still full to the top.

"Oh, don't you care for mint juleps?" I asked.

She replied in excellent English: "Last night I was told that your Southern drink is very strong. I decided not to risk missing your national birthday after coming so far to be here."

The next morning we drove the royal couple to Jamestown. They asked if the motorcade

TWO DECADES BEFORE HIS EXECUTION IN ROMANIA, PRESIDENT CEAUSESCU PLAYED
VOLLEYBALL WITH HIS WIFE AND OTHERS IN WILLIAMSBURG.

could stop at a turnout on the Jamestown-Yorktown Parkway. The Thais got out of the limousine, took off their shoes and walked a quarter of a mile or so into a field of Queen Anne's lace. Before they left for Washington, another folksy scene occurred at the Capitol on the Duke of Gloucester Street. The King, an avid photographer, stepped out on a tiny balcony to take some pictures. American-Thai relations advanced in a major way when photographs were sent around the world of the King taking pictures of the friendly crowd below, who, in turn, were taking pictures of the King.

When the news came from Romania in 1989 that President Nikolae Ceausescu and his wife had been executed as "enemies of the people," we recalled their visit to the colonial capital years before. The Romanian couple was exceptionally low-key then. When Carl Humelsine asked the Romanian leader what sports he enjoyed, the answer was surprisingly, "volleyball." Humelsine quietly flashed the word to Dick Sessoms, who used a walkie-talkie to summon a net and ball from The College of William and Mary. When the Romanian and his entourage returned to their official accommodations after their walk along the Duke of Gloucester Street, the volleyball equipment was in place in the yard of the Lightfoot House, then the official VIP residence.

A pickup game with Romanians on one side of the net and State Department and Colonial Williamsburg "players," including Mary Humesline, on the other was quickly formed.

It was soon clear why the Romanian foreign minister had lasted thirteen years in his post. He never hit the ball over the net; he always set it up for the President. When Norman Beatty of Colonial Williamsburg blocked a hard shot by the Romanian leader, a U.S. Secret Service agent whispered, "In Romania you would be executed for that!"

We were the perfect hosts as the Romanians edged ahead of the U.S. "team" by fifteen to two. But the game ended when the ranking American player, U.S. Deputy Chief of Protocol Bill Codus, split the seat of his trousers during one high leap. A quick caucus determined there was no way to mend the ripped pants. As we had no substitutes, the Romanians were declared the winners, and the official visit was off to an inspired start.

In its next issue, *Life* magazine printed the photo of Codus's partially exposed backside as its choice for "The Picture of the Week!"

From these visits, Williamsburg and State got to know each other well. On one occasion Secretary of State Dean Rusk came to Williamsburg to deliver a major address, and as soon as he completed his remarks he slipped away to the Golden Horseshoe Golf Course at the Williamsburg Inn for a quick round of golf with his fellow Colonial Williamsburg Trustee, George Seaton of Hollywood. It was a tight squeeze time-wise as Rusk had to fly to Brussels that evening to attend an international conference.

Nevertheless, after the golf game Rusk, his Secret Service agent and I had time for a quick lunch at the golf club. I had known Rusk when I was the diplomatic correspondent for the United Press at the State Department some years before.

"Dean," I said, smiling, "do you ever get away from this guy (the Secret Service agent)?"

"Oh sure," the Secretary replied. "Not long ago, when I was the target of a lot of criticism on Capitol Hill, I slipped away with my wife in our old Chevrolet and went to a drive-in for a barbecue and a milk shake. The carhop was taking my order when he looked down, and said, 'Hey you sure do look a lot like the Secretary of State.' I said, 'Don't you dare compare me with *that guy.*'

"'What's the matter with you,' the carhop retorted, 'I think he's a good guy.'"

Rusk declared, "That kid made my day! Of course, I did not tell him who I really was."

Another time he gave the Secret Service the slip on a Sunday evening. He told us how he gathered up the laundry, picked up a detective novel, got some quarters and drove off alone in the old Chevy to a local laundromat.

"Nobody would ever expect the Secretary of State to be in a laundromat," Rusk said, laughing. "I did all the wash, and read there alone for forty-five minutes. No one recognized me. That, too, made my day."

When Queen Elizabeth II and His Royal Highness Prince Philip visited the United States in October 1957, the couple's visit to Jamestown, tea at The College of William and Mary and a tour and dinner at Colonial Williamsburg took less than twenty-four hours, including a night's sleep. Local observers estimated that Williamsburg's biggest crowd ever, ranging up to 35,000, lined the Duke of Gloucester Street to welcome the royal couple.

All went well until the Queen completed her remarks to a large crowd gathered in the College Yard in front of the Wren Building. Winthrop and Mrs. Rockefeller were standing by with horses and a carriage to escort the royalty down the Duke of Gloucester Street past Bruton Parish Church to the Governor's Palace. Soldiers from Fort Knox, Kentucky, lined

SECRETARY OF STATE DEAN RUSK HEADS FOR THE GOLF COURSE WITH GEORGE
SEATON, THE HOLLYWOOD DIRECTOR AND COLONIAL WILLIAMSBURG TRUSTEE.

the street as one of many precautions against any incident. Officials of Colonial Williamsburg were apprehensive that the huge crowd and photographers' flash bulbs might frighten
the horses pulling the VIP carriage. Therefore, to guard against any equine upsets Jake
Keyser, in charge of Colonial Williamsburg's horses, called in a veterinarian that morning
to calm the horses with injections of thorazine, a sedative administered in horse-sized
amounts.

The experiment worked all too well. After the VIPs were seated in the carriage and ready
to go, nothing happened. The horses didn't move. It took a few quick and forceful snaps of
their bridles to bring the horses out of their fog before they moved forward—slightly "lop-
legged," as one observer put it.

At the time of the royal visit my wife and I were still living in Washington, a year away
from our move to Williamsburg. We received an engraved invitation from Secretary of State

HER MAJESTY QUEEN ELIZABETH,
QUEEN MOTHER OF ENGLAND, ON HER
WAY TO SEE THE GOVERNOR'S PALACE
IN 1954 WITH KENNETH CHORLEY,
PRESIDENT OF WILLIAMSBURG.

QUEEN ELIZABETH II AND PRINCE
PHILIP SPENT TWENTY-FOUR
WHIRLWIND HOURS IN 1957 SEEING
JAMESTOWN, TAKING TEA AT WILLIAM
AND MARY, TOURING CW AND DINING
WITH WINTHROP ROCKEFELLER.

John Foster Dulles and Mrs. Dulles to attend a white-tie reception and dinner in honor of the royal visitors from England. The protocol in 1957 required the diplomatic correspondents of the United Press (my job), the Associated Press and the International News Service to represent the media at State dinners. Wives were always invited, too.

The formal dinner, held in the ballroom of the Pan American Union, was very special. The head table was placed at one end of the ballroom with two long flanking tables extending toward a stage where the U.S. Air Force Strings played. I was seated next to commentator Lowell Thomas and Mrs. Clement E. Conger, the perky and pretty wife of the Deputy Chief of Protocol.

The pièce de résistance for the evening's entertainment was an ill-fated dance written, choreographed and performed by Marge and Gower Champion. The audience anticipated a great show as the talented pair started their act. Their dance was called *Country Fair*. After twirling gracefully, the Champions paused to pantomime the familiar sledgehammer and bell act.

Gower Champion swung the imaginary sledge, but there was no responding ring. After several silent swings, Marge tapped Gower on the shoulder, motioned him aside and swung the sledge in an exaggerated gesture, looking up to signal the percussionist. At last, the bell rang! As the two continued the dance the audience noticed that one of Marge's straps had popped loose from the front of her gown and was bobbing on her back. Gower deftly stuffed it under the top of her dress.

Moments later, the dancers stopped to perform the sledge and bell act again. As they danced away, the other strap popped loose. This time Marge pushed the dangling strap into her bosom.

Suddenly the dancers stopped, and Gower said to the white-tie guests: "Marge and I have looked forward to this evening for many months. Her dress was made especially for this event. But as you have seen Marge and her dress have parted company—so must we part company with you."

Official dinners in the Historic Area or at Carter's Grove Plantation were usually good for a laugh. On one occasion in 1954, recalled in her memoirs, Mrs. Kenneth Chorley, wife of the second President of Colonial Williamsburg, had a tête-à-tête with Queen Elizabeth, the Queen Mother. After feasting at a King's Arms Tavern table with Winthrop Rockefeller and Williamsburg Mayor Henry M. ("Polly") Stryker, it was "my job," reported Mrs. Chorley, "to take the Queen Mother . . . to the ladies' room because we were going on a candlelight tour of the Capitol this evening.

"When we got to the powder room, the Queen Mother said to me, 'Mrs. Chorley, is this the Mr. Rockefeller [Winthrop] who's been having such difficulty with his marriage?'

"And I said, 'Yes, ma'am, it is.'

"'And,' she asked, 'He has been divorced?'

"I said, 'Yes ma'am.'

"'And with an enormous settlement?'

"'Yes, Your Majesty,' I said, 'about seven million dollars.'

"And she said, 'Oh, poor man!'

"And then the Queen Mother said, 'Well, we've had our little gossip.'"

PRIME MINISTER INDIRA GANDHI
OF INDIA HAD HER OFFICIAL CARRIAGE
RIDE WITH CHIEF OF PROTOCOL
JAMES SYMINGTON, DOWN
FROM WASHINGTON TO MEET HER.

PRINCE CHARLES'S VISIT FOLLOWED
HIS PARENTS' AND GRANDMOTHER'S
IN 1981. HE SAW THE GOVERNOR'S
PALACE IN THE COMPANY OF
CHIEF CURATOR HOOD (LEFT) AND
GOVERNOR JOHN DALTON.

THE SHAH OF IRAN IS ONLY ONE
OF MANY HEADS OF STATE WHO HAVE
COME TO SEE HISTORIC
WILLIAMSBURG, BUT HE IS EASILY THE
MOST ROYAL LOOKING OF THEM ALL.

LISTENING INTENTLY TO A
DESCRIPTION OF COLONIAL
PAPERMAKING BY CRAFTSMAN CLEM
SANFORD IS KING HUSSEIN OF JORDAN.
THE KING'S VISIT WAS IN 1973.

TWENTIETH-CENTURY
POLITICAL/ECONOMIC SUMMIT
LEADERS FROM AROUND THE WORLD
POSED AGAINST THE RECONSTRUCTED
COLONIAL CAPITOL.

CHANCELLOR HELMUT KOHL OF WEST
GERMANY, ARRIVING FOR THE SUMMIT
MEETING IN 1983, STEPS FROM
A HELICOPTER TO A HORSE-DRAWN
CARRIAGE IN THE CW TRADITION.

THE CARRIAGE MET ALL 'COPTERS
BRINGING VIPS TO THE SUMMIT
MEETING. HERE THE RECEPTION
GROUP WELCOMES JAPANESE PRIME
MINISTER NAKASONE.

"PLEASE FOLLOW ME," SAYS
GONZALES, DIRECTING VIPS FROM
AUSTRALIA. PRIME MINISTER GOUGH
WHITLAM IS IN THE SECOND TIER
BEHIND THE POLKA-DOT SCARF.

WILLIAMSBURG AND RICHMOND

The restoration progressing at Williamsburg became a matter of growing pride to the Commonwealth of Virginia. And when statesmen and women from all over the world began visiting the old colonial capital, appreciation for the project deepened. This good feeling gradually grew into a partnership that, in effect, made Williamsburg an informal arm of the state's government. The teamwork was of tremendous value to Colonial Williamsburg, too, as we grappled with issues like highway signs and construction, travel, promotion and development, advertising, cultural liaisons, governors' conferences and many other major projects.

Governor Thomas B. Stanley once commented that the millions of dollars generated by travel to Williamsburg through gasoline taxes alone were enough to pay for the restoration. The fact that *all* the money was provided by John D. Rockefeller, Jr., made the growing attraction even more valuable.

Virginia's high regard for Rockefeller was expressed soon after the restoration activities began. In 1934, the Commonwealth's General Assembly traveled from Richmond to Williamsburg to hold a commemorative session where its first sessions had been held in the 1700s. On this occasion, the Virginia legislature made Rockefeller an honorary citizen of Virginia and commissioned a painting of him to be placed in the Virginia State Capitol.

On our home grounds, Colonial Williamsburg also enjoyed excellent and mutually beneficial relations with the Williamsburg City Council and James City and York County governments. Cooperative ventures such as sealing off streets to recapture the colonial atmosphere, restricting traffic, changing ordinances to control signs and set other regulations, and transferring important property were all carried on quietly and smoothly for the most part. Relations with mayors of the old city were particularly good, for where else would small-town officials be called out of their dental and legal offices to greet heads of state from scores of foreign countries? This happened as often as twice in one day on a few occasions, but usually VIP arrivals occurred at least twice a month during the years Williamsburg was an overnight stop from abroad to the White House.

THE SIGN OF THE BLUE BELL TAVERN, WHERE THE AUTHOR STAYED ON HIS ARRIVAL IN WILLIAMSBURG IN 1958, FRAMES WILLIAMSBURG'S CAPITOL.

A CARRIAGE RIDE ALONG THE DUKE OF GLOUCESTER STREET CONJURES
UP THE BEAUTY, SIMPLICITY AND DEMOCRATIC WAYS OF COLONIAL LIFE IN AMERICA.

The Richmond-Williamsburg liaison had all the aspects of an appropriate and legitimate romance sans a marriage—that would have been *too* close. We talked almost daily with the politicians who drove the engines of power. We were available under Carl Humelsine's direction to help the state and city in myriad social, economic, cultural and political efforts (the latter was touchy because of Colonial Williamsburg's non-profit status). We did not as an organization engage in political campaigns, but as private individuals we supported efforts that concerned Colonial Williamsburg's welfare. For example, on one occasion Richmond sponsors engaged a New York public relations firm to lobby Virginia into offering liquor-by-the-drink instead of only by the bottle in state stores. We favored that thirst-quenching legislation because travelers usually expected liquor to be easily available. But we sat on the sidelines and watched the campaign for new legislation fail. The first test vote went flat in a General Assembly committee, sixteen to zero! Yet liquor sales at state-controlled stores near the Richmond Capitol enjoyed the highest sales of spirits ever, mostly to legislators from other parts of the state. When confronted with the statistics, the lawmakers ascribed the high sales to lobbyists and the press.

After most of the wounds of that staggering (and sobering) defeat healed, the effort for legalizing liquor-by-the-drink began again, this time quietly without New York promotion. With professional lobbying based in Richmond, we joined with the travel industry to explain that for bars and restaurants to compete effectively for travel dollars eliminating the ban on mixed drinks was only one of a number of moves the Commonwealth had to make to promote tourism. No resistance came from the clergy, the Women's Christian Temperance Union, etc. The measure passed handily, and Williamsburg became the second area in Virginia to approve local option to serve drinks.

While the Richmond debate was going on I received a telephone call from the Williamsburg Inn desk. The clerk said, "David Brinkley just arrived. We did not expect him as the reservation was under A. Brinkley."

I called Brinkley's room and his wife said, "He is so tired, we wanted to get away from Washington for a few days. When we signed in at 5:45 P.M. we realized we were in Virginia and couldn't buy a drink. David got back into the car to try to get to the ABC store before 6. He was furious!" I was glad to be able to tell the Brinkleys the drought would last only a couple of weeks more.

As the restoration of Colonial Williamsburg moved ahead, we frequently received telephone calls from the Governor requesting "volunteers" for many interesting projects.

Governor Mills E. Godwin, Jr., forever a gentleman, was a true friend of Williamsburg and recognized as an outstanding Virginia leader. He was so popular he was elected Governor as a Democrat in 1965 and as a Republican in 1973.

Godwin called one day to report he was planning a trade mission to several Western European nations, and he needed some ideas on gifts he could present to his hosts. We agreed on Williamsburg tea caddies, beautifully crafted eighteenth-century-style mahogany boxes. Upon his return from Europe, Governor Godwin called to say how surprised he was to find that none of the ministers of trade he met knew much about Virginia, "but they all knew about Williamsburg." Our fame was due, of course, to the many visits made by heads of state to the Historic Area.

Soon after beginning my job in Williamsburg I began preparing a list of prominent Virginians I should get to know for professional reasons. Among those on top was former Virginia Governor Colgate Darden, whom I found in his Norfolk retirement office. He was extremely candid and helpful. He spoke openly of his objections to the method adopted to finance the Chesapeake Bay Bridge Tunnel, a seventeen-mile link between the Virginia shore at Norfolk and the Eastern Shore. To maintain the appearance of following Virginia's policy of "pay as you go" (never borrowing!), the government established separate authority to issue revenue bonds supported only by toll income.

"Everyone knew," he said, "that Virginia would back the bonds, if necessary. It would have saved Virginia many, many millions of dollars if the huge project had been backed instead by general obligation bonds. But the other way made it appear that 'pay as you go' was in effect."

After explaining in more detail the philosophy and operation of Governor Harry F. Byrd's political-financial dynasty, Darden made a memorable comment about Colonial Williamsburg. Noting that John D. Rockefeller, Jr., was a "New Yorker, an outsider, a non-Virginian," Darden said: "It's really a good thing Colonial Williamsburg didn't fall into the hands of the Virginians [he was a Virginian born in Southhampton County]; we would have put up plaques all over the place."

Without disrespect to his native Commonwealth, he cited the "old church at Jamestown" to support his comment on plaques. With a jolly laugh he observed, "If it weren't for all those plaques on the walls of the church it would have fallen down years ago!"

Darden said Virginia governors regarded the Maryland-born President of Colonial Williamsburg as an accomplished executive who knew how to get things done. Humelsine understood the Virginia political scene and, with Darden and others, admired Carter O. Lowance, a former journalist and sage adviser to six Commonwealth governors. For his quiet manner and effective counsel, Carter was known as "Virginia's Little Governor." Old hands relied heavily on him, as did Humelsine when he dealt at the state level. Through these and other connections, Humelsine was made head of many Virginia commissions and boards. As a result, Colonial Williamsburg played a leading role in the Virginia Museum of Fine Arts, Conservation and Economic Development Board, Governor's Conference on Natural Beauty, Committee for Better Roads in Virginia (to get support to raise the gasoline tax) and the controversy between the Virginia Museum of Fine Arts and the Governor's office. The museum was in the position of determining distribution of federal money for state art projects at the same time it was seeking some of the same funds. In most other states, these delicate and important functions were handled by separate arts councils. Humelsine and two other Colonial Williamsburg Trustees—Webster Rhoads and Morton Thalhimer—were also trustees of the Virginia Museum of Fine Arts.

Against this background, Governor Godwin asked me to serve on a special commission to create a separate arts council for the state. Recognizing how awkward the position could be with three of my own bosses serving as museum trustees, I asked for time before answering. I consulted with Humelsine, who unequivocally told me, "Volunteer!" To his credit and that of Rhodes and Thalhimer they never sought in any way to influence me after I accepted the appointment. The museum did not relinquish its authority easily, but the proposal to create a Virginia Commission of the Arts and Humanities was finally approved by the Virginia General Assembly. My sensitive position was not relieved, however, as Governor Godwin then appointed me to the new commission, and I was promptly selected as first chairman. Humelsine told me to "volunteer" again. Seven years later I was relieved of the statewide arts job.

One significant incident stands out from the early days of the arts and humanities task force. "Brud" Holland, President of Hampton University who became U.S. Ambassador to

Sweden and later a member of the New York Stock Exchange, was a commission member, and we frequently traveled together to attend meetings.

On one plane trip to Roanoke, Holland and I talked about a project we wanted to initiate, a school for gifted youngsters. Holland cautioned that this move should not be the commission's only priority. The needs of the underprivileged should have at least equal ranking, if not higher. He put it this way:

"Think of the little black boy in southside Virginia who might hear about a new school for the gifted. Might he not say, 'Yes, but what are you doing for me?'"

I repeated Holland's view at the commission meeting. It gave us new perception and balance as we went to work.

Because of Humelsine's growing stature in Virginia and his previous background at the State Department, President Johnson appointed him as the first chairman of the U.S. Bicentennial Commission. This prestigious assignment swept Colonial Williamsburg into the national scene. We were in "at the creation," dealing with government agencies to find Washington office space, chairs, desks, pencils, paper, etc. Meetings of the new commission followed, and plans for the nation's 200th birthday were under way. However, soon after Richard Nixon became President, Humelsine heard he would be replaced by a Canadian-born Californian, a friend of the new President. Naively, we had not expected the nation's birthday planning to be a political plum. But it was so regarded by the new administration.

Soon after Humelsine's status was reduced to vice chairman, he resigned for a "combination of many circumstances." In a ten-line reply Nixon expressed his thanks for Humelsine's "efforts and cooperation."

Several years later, columnist James Jackson Kilpatrick wrote that the American Revolutionary Bicentennial Commission "is floundering badly. Lyndon Johnson put some good people on the first commission, notably Carl Humelsine of Colonial Williamsburg, but Nixon lopped them off in favor of political appointees." Kilpatrick concluded, "Tories are now officially in charge of producing the Grand and Glorious Fizzle of 1976."

Humelsine had long since withdrawn from the Bicentennial scene, fading back in the mists of Colonial Williamsburg.

During all the years of "volunteering," Colonial Williamsburg gained extraordinary experience and important contacts on a high and influential scale. In large part, Humelsine made this opportunity possible through his executive clout and ability to delegate to top aides, curators, interior designers, historians, preservation and conservation experts, architects and other skilled professionals in their individual fields.

When outside demands became onerous and we wondered how any of us got our own homework done, we recalled the story told by a British speaker at the Williamsburg Antiques Forum. It was about a woman in Bath, England, who had given birth to twins. When she came home and invited the ladies of the neighborhood to see the double products, she said proudly, "My doctor says twins happen only once in 332,644 times!" One of her listeners was overwhelmed at the thought and, after catching her breath, blurted, "Nelly, I just don't see how you ever had time to do your housework!"

Our double life at Williamsburg was absorbing, creative and rewarding, and somehow we all found time both to "volunteer" and to do our "housework" at home.

LIGHTER MOMENTS
BEHIND THE SCENES

As the VIPs passed by with all of their frills and pressures, you can bet there was another side to the coin. Quietly, we posted a watch for dollops of humor or byplay, mainly of our own doing uninspired by diplomats and other outsiders. I kept a casual file of some of the better tension-easers that served all of us well:

Who would have guessed that Chinese was once spoken in the highest Colonial Williamsburg circles?

Or that a colonial Mercedes went berserk and nearly finished off a promising management career in colonial restoration?

Or that a Governor of Virginia and a colonial executive teamed up one night, long after normal business hours, to build a road around Williamsburg?

The first of the hitherto undisclosed stories began to unfold when a Colonial Williamsburg computer operator made a grim mistake. This was predictable, I guess, at the time we were moving out of colonial pencil-and-quill office procedures into the perils of computers. The slip-up was more than embarrassing as it occurred in a routine fund-raising letter, the first issued by Charles R. Longsworth, Colonial Williamsburg's new President succeeding Humelsine. Furthermore, the mistake was addressed to one of our best-loved, retired Trustees—Armistead Boothe, a most prominent Virginian and former candidate for Lieutenant Governor of the Commonwealth. The form letter began:

Mr. Armistead Boot He
913 Vicar Lane
Alexandria, VA 22302

Dear Mr. He:

As Colonial Williamsburg's new president, I am delighted to learn of your recent visit. [Boothe not only had been a Trustee of Colonial Williamsburg, he had visited Williamsburg probably 100 times in forty years!] Your interest and support are welcome, and I hope you will return soon.

Please be as generous as you can. Thank you very much. . . .

IN HIS OFFICE, THE FOURTH PRESIDENT OF COLONIAL WILLIAMSBURG, CHARLES R. LONGSWORTH, HEARS GOOD NEWS OVER THE TELEPHONE.

Boothe, now and forever "Boot He," had a deft sense of humor. Thus armed and inspired, he did not miss the opportunity to use it:

Dear Mr. Longsworth:

About seex weeks ago, I gotta your letter of May 2, 1978. Puleez scuse me for not write sooner but it took me 4 week to get some Chinese money from New York.

As you recall from a your letter I am Boot He, the first Chinese I believe to get letter from the great President of Williamsburg. So that you remember me, I am send you copy of you letter to me, of envelop in which it was enclose and also copy of you sad plea which break my heart and make me glad to get the Chinese money.

Since I want to do all I can for you and the Challenge: '78, I do here send you name of one of my best frien who is Arab Prince and has lotsa money. Hees name is Lewis Pow Ell.* He hass as much brain as money so he is feelthy reech. Puleez write him and ask for some middle east money or perhaps some oil wells. Don't believe him if he say he is po.

Weeth bes wish and hope for suckcessfool campaign, I am

Yours,
Armistead Boot He

[*Lewis Powell, Trustee and Chairman of Colonial Williamsburg, our former General Counsel and Associate Justice of the Supreme Court of the United States]

Longsworth, after long reflection, decided to stick with his tricky new job, and responded:

Dear Mr. He:

May I call you Boot?

I certainly enjoyed your letter and appreciate your interest. Your reply gave special pleasure to Mr. Rogert Thal Her, our Cambodian development officer, who is glad to know of another Oriental person interested in Colonial Williamsburg, the home of Chinese Chippendale. Mr. Her has made special mention of your interesting and generous response to one of the key punch operators, whose name is Mu Ud.

I wrote to Mr. Ell who replied as follows: he is too busy talking with all his friends in medical school admissions offices to bother with a place without any quotas; he is now known in his profession as a 'swinger'; he knows no Hes, but once went to school with an Armistead, whose interest was in Shes. I assume that rules out youse.

At any rate (or price) we have a yen for your cash and an opportunity to meet you sometime.

Yours,
s/ Charles R. Longsworth

From his sheltered retirement dugout Humelsine couldn't resist getting into the "Chinese" fray. He addressed an official communique to all Trustees of Colonial Williamsburg, as follows:

THE COLONIAL WILLIAMSBURG FOUNDATION

Williamsburg, Virginia
August 24, 1978

To: Honorable Trustees
From: Chairman Hu Mel Sine

As your humble servant, I beg to inform you of progress in ancient institution of Colonial Williamsburg.

During full moon-lotus season on advice of consultant we traded in quills for new computer that writes letters, sends bills, answers complaints, and types very fast, "That Fut Ure May Earn From Past"—sometimes very well.

Computer so far has some sweet-sour days, some bugs and egg drop in it. This is revealed in enclosed exchange of letters between computer and Mr. Armistead Boot He, Chinese gentleman, and voracious President Longsworth.

Computer is important, I am told, as it has tea leaf and ricey capability to roll in much yen. Happily, Mr. Boot He has aimed it at Lewis Pow Ell.

Boor Stin, B. Rinkley, B. Yrd and Wan Ton Sea Ton are next!

With prospect of campaign plenty suckcessfool Board meeting in Year of Goat will most likely be in Shanghai. Please puttee book and we will see you there, Honorable Trust Hes (and Shes). Mr. Boot He says he has but fifty-one summers and is petitioning for Board membership so keep in mind that Confucius say, "Soul that is retired often attempts to return clothed in new form."

Mr. Sine

Mr. Daniel J. Boorstin
Mr. David Brinkley
Mr. Richard E. Byrd
Mr. Joseph C. Carter, Jr.
Mr. Joseph F. Cullman 3rd
Mr. J. Richardson Dilworth
Mr. Ralph W. Ellison
Mrs. Seth M. Hufstedler
Mr. L. William Lane, Jr.
Mr. Charles R. Longsworth
Mr. T. Justin Moore, Jr.
Mrs. George D. O'Neill
Mr. George D. O'Neill
Mr. George Putnam
Mr. Donald K. Ross
Mr. George Seaton
Mr. Edgar F. Shannon, Jr.
Mr. Alan Simpson

Another one for the file developed when Carl and Mary Humelsine went to Europe one summer, leaving me in charge of major surgery and repairs on Carl's cherished Mercedes. I had long been regarded by Humelsine as "Seaman 79," the highest rating I ever attained as "a hand" on his boat, hence this "directive" which arrived after they departed for Europe:

To: Seaman 79
From: C. H. Humelsine

In order to keep you out of trouble during Mary's absence [in Michigan] and to give you some point of interest, I am assigning a small project to your capable hands while we are away.

My Mercedes has several ailments:

(1) The clutch does not work properly.

(2) Nobody seems to be able to make the air conditioning work for more than a short period.

(3) The chrome around the exhaust needs attention.

(4) There is a certain noise that is utterly foreign to the normal smooth-running motor.

I should like very much to have all these items corrected when I return, and with your capability I have no doubt that this can be accomplished. I hope you will not give up until you have successfully eliminated the above problems.

C. H. H.

P.S. We have every intention of upgrading your rating upon the successful completion of this mission. M & C H

I fired up the convertible the next day and drove it to "Karl's—Specialist in European Cars." I gave "Karl" a copy of the "Seaman 79" memorandum, told him he had four weeks to do the job and went back to work. Three weeks later, just to be sure everything was going okay, I drove by. The Mercedes was sitting exactly where I had left it! The reason: "The parts are coming from New Jersey." I told Karl we had only a week before Carl would be home; fast action was imperative, and I would be back in a week to get the repaired Mercedes as it was the key to my future. On the day of expected delivery, two hours before Humelsine was due home, I went by the shop. Karl shook his head—still no clutch or exhaust chrome, the air conditioning was stubborn, and the engine was still noisy. Woe was us and, particularly, *me*.

I decided to have that car in Carl's parking lot, nevertheless, along with a detailed accounting of the other Karl's "failures." So I started the Mercedes back to Williamsburg, three miles away. As I checked the dash I noted (1) the gasoline tank was on "empty," and (2) the Virginia state inspection sticker had expired, making it illegal to drive the blasted car. Therefore, I took a quick and quiet back road to Roy Rhodes's service station on Richmond Road. Though it was late, he inspected the Mercedes and it passed. But I lost a precious hour.

As I knew, the automobile usually was serviced by Texaco at the Williamsburg Information Center. I gambled and made it there on "empty." But while I was distracted a Texaco serviceman filled the car with twenty-two gallons of diesel fuel instead of gasoline! I didn't

THE TEAM WHO MADE WILLIAMSBURG THE "U.S. DEPARTMENT OF STATE SOUTH":
PRESIDENT CARL HUMELSINE AND SENIOR VICE PRESIDENT DONALD GONZALES.

know this until I started to leave. The convertible rolled about twenty feet and expired. It wouldn't start. An observant attendant finally said, "Maybe it uses gas." That it did.

We hoisted the Mercedes on the grease rack, loosened the gas tank plug with all the wrong tools, dumped twenty-two gallons of fuel down the drain, filled the tank with twenty-two gallons of gasoline and called Karl to get advice on starting it up. He suggested disconnecting spark plugs and putting gasoline in each cylinder. It sounded like a sure explosion! I could see bits and pieces of flaming Mercedes blown skyward. Karl said not to worry, "The diesel left in there will make it run the best ever."

While an attendant sat behind the wheel to keep the car going, I called home and said to Mary, "You know we have talked about early retirement; it may be tonight. Come to Texaco and follow me down the Jamestown Parkway. I have to test-hop the Mercedes. Carl can't be ten minutes from home, hurry. And bring a Scotch and soda!" As we went down the parkway the Mercedes belched huge clouds of diesel smoke laced with gasoline. Finally it cleared up. We parked the car at Humelsine's house, put the keys through the door slot and fled the scene to another Scotch and soda, or more.

The next morning the telephone rang. It was Humelsine.

"When we got home last night, I had to go to the 7-11 for milk and bread," he said. "What did you do to that car? It never ran better. The engine noise is gone. It sounded great! Congratulations."

I accepted the kudos graciously, not quite knowing what to say, so I offered, "Well, old friend, you can always count on me to handle the tough ones! Since the mission is so successful, do you want to tell me now what you meant about upgrading my rating?" Response, "Upgrade what?" I let it go.

Later that morning at the office I recounted the problems that never quite turned into opportunities and suggested to my boss he might want to buy an American car. To my great relief he merely denounced Texaco for charging him for twenty-two gallons of down-the-drain diesel. After long, intense debates Texaco reluctantly agreed to a rebate, and the case of the Mercedes faded at last into the haze of other crises.

Despite funny forays into computers, Mercedes and other sallies, my favorite Williamsburg behind-the-scenes story centers on how a Virginia Governor, during a night-time telephone call, neatly trapped a reluctant Humelsine into taking on direction of a major public service project.

The telephone rang one night about 10:00 P.M. at Humelsine's residence. It was Virginia Governor Linwood Holton speaking:

"Carl, I'm having trouble with Jinks (Holton's sparkling wife)," the Governor said.

"Why are you calling me? I'm sure I can't help you, Linwood," Humelsine observed wryly.

"Well," Holton said, "when Attorney General John Mitchell and Martha Mitchell were here for my inauguration, Martha stormed in the front door of the mansion and declared, 'Well, Jinks, it's just beautiful, but where in the hell are the antiques?' Jinks agrees with Martha, and says I ought to do something about it! What was that you recently told me about your friend Henry Green, who headed up a citizens' committee to furnish the Governor's Mansion in Atlanta?"

Humelsine said the project, accomplished by "citizen volunteers," had been a huge success in Georgia and would be an excellent pattern for Virginia to follow in upgrading the second oldest executive mansion in continuous use in the United States.

"Carl, I hoped you'd say that . . . I want you to agree to chair a similar citizens' committee here in Virginia," Holton said.

Humelsine backed off quickly, protesting that he was already overburdened with too many projects. The Governor was undeterred and quickly played his trump card—an irresistible quid pro quo.

"What was that you told me the other day, Carl, about wanting a bypass around Williamsburg to relieve downtown traffic in the Historic Area?" Holton asked confidently. The offer was obvious and Carl took the bait.

Holton, whose wife was carefully monitoring the conversation, reported to her with great relief, "The mansion will be upgraded soon!" At his end, Carl relaxed, never guessing he would not be relieved from his "volunteer" job for many years. In fact, the bypass was opened to traffic halfway around Williamsburg long before Humelsine was retired from the project ten years later by Governor John Dalton.

A RACE WITH RACE RELATIONS

For twenty-five years, Colonial Williamsburg's day-to-day operations covered every possible economic, political and social issue in addition to the more glamorous task of entertaining VIPs from home and abroad. An ordinary day could include conversations with the White House, State Department, the Mayor of Williamsburg, the Governor of Virginia, a member of Congress, a local church or civic group. All the grim issues of twentieth-century America seemed to have some Williamsburg relevance that traced back to eighteenth-century roots.

One of the critical issues was a continuing race with race relations. Stemming from the earliest days of slavery in the colony of Virginia, racial tensions hovered over the Rockefellers, Colonial Williamsburg and the City of Williamsburg for many years. The search for ways to mollify the situation was always a challenge as the local society, prodded by rapid change resulting from the Williamsburg restoration, moved from the misty past to the dynamic present.

When we arrived in Williamsburg in 1958, segregation in schools and public places was still in effect in Virginia, a fact of life that affected Colonial Williamsburg in many ways. Both the restoration project and The College of William and Mary employed a large number of blacks, many of whom had children in local schools. Also, Colonial Williamsburg operated restaurants, two theaters, swimming pools and several hotels and taverns. "Jim Crow" practices in Williamsburg, including segregated restrooms, were the same as elsewhere in the Deep South. The situation was clearly at odds with the Rockefeller philosophy of supporting minorities, especially in educational endeavors.

Before my family arrived in Williamsburg in the early summer of 1958, I stayed in the Market Square Tavern and ate most of my meals at the Williamsburg Lodge. One Sunday, I sat on the Lodge porch after dinner. A nicely dressed lady and her daughter walked by, stopped and engaged in an animated discussion with a local taxi driver. When they walked away, I asked the driver if the Lodge guests were upset about something.

"Yeah," he drawled. "They said they're 'feeding Negroes in there.' 'Hell,' I said, 'they been feeding Negroes in there for years.'"

John D. Rockefeller 3rd, when he was Chairman of The Colonial Williamsburg Board in

A FRIENDLY NEIGHBOR WHO ENJOYED PARTICIPATING IN COMMUNITY LIFE,
JOHN D. ROCKEFELLER, JR., VISITS WITH ALEX PLEASANTS, BRUTON PARISH SEXTON.

1949, decided to desegregate Colonial Williamsburg's facilities notwithstanding Virginia customs and laws. After Rockefeller sought their advice, three distinguished Virginians said Colonial Williamsburg could feed and house blacks "in a separate wing" if they were part of a group, but they warned that the Commonwealth would not tolerate hotels that registered blacks in general.

This reaction did not satisfy Rockefeller. He drafted a statement:

> In answer to questions we have been asked by many people, we now therefore say that all who come here to draw inspiration from this Restoration will be welcomed and housed and fed in the facilities of Colonial Williamsburg without regard to race, creed or color.

Years later, I heard that a further part of the 1949 plan had been for John 3rd to read that statement for public consumption in the Hall of the House of Burgesses. However, this was not done.

John 3rd's advocacy of moving ahead of Virginia on black rights caused real problems with his father, who, like his son, had deep pro-minority, liberal feelings on the issue. Regardless of his instincts, John, Jr., felt the only way to go at the time was to abide by the Commonwealth's customs and rules. He made a key change in the statement, therefore, to make it read that everyone would be welcomed and fed and housed "insofar as that is reasonably possible"—gone was "without regard to race, creed or color." This irritated the son, who was still Chairman of Colonial Williamsburg's Board, and the conflict of views was yet another factor that brought about John 3rd's decision to resign as Chairman three years later.

As racial barriers gradually weakened in the 1950s and 1960s, we found ourselves grappling more and more with the consequences of segregation. Desegregation was clearly imminent but not without the growing pains of all concerned.

For example, a black minister telephoned me one day to say that he and his family wanted to see *To Kill a Mockingbird* in the Williamsburg Theatre (operated by Colonial Williamsburg). However, he did not intend to sit in the area traditionally roped off for blacks as required by state law. I replied that Colonial Williamsburg, without publicity, had already removed the barriers and that the family could sit anywhere they wished.

In advance of the change in the segregation law, we sought the advice of Lewis F. Powell, Jr., a Trustee and General Counsel of Colonial Williamsburg before he joined the United States Supreme Court. We needed his counsel regarding the admission to the Visitor's Center, which was free of charge for everyone. His advice was to go ahead quietly and desegregate the Williamsburg Theatre since the law was going to change soon.

Events nearly overcame us, and we soon knew we weren't through with this sensitive issue. Through a liaison with The College of William and Mary and Hampton University, we heard that the step-daughter of British writer C. P. Snow, a student in Williamsburg, was participating in plans to spark a student march on behalf of human rights. One of the targets was said to be the Colonial Williamsburg Theatre located on the Duke of Gloucester Street, nearer than a stone's throw from the campus. It was true. Carloads of black and white students arrived in the parking lot one evening with placards denouncing Colonial Williamsburg. We knew they were coming. Three bought tickets and went into the movie, expecting to find a roped-off area for blacks. Not only were there no ropes but no ushers to enforce restricted seating. After five minutes, the students left the theater to tell their cohorts there was nothing to picket for.

A more harrowing incident occurred during the spring tour of the Harvard Glee Club. David Rockefeller, Jr., was the president of the male singers. Of course, we wanted everything to go smoothly although we were quite aware that there could be racial problems. We worked hard to prepare the community. My wife and I took in three students at our house, the Robert Carter House adjacent to the Governor's Palace, including one black graduate student from Mississippi. Glee Club tours of the Historic Area went smoothly. But at intermission during the concert on the William and Mary campus, I received word in the balcony that Dean Mel Jones wanted to see me backstage, pronto!

As I rounded the stage, I could see a crisis was under way. College and Glee Club representatives looked very grim. I soon learned that at least one black student had been refused food at the privately owned Campus Restaurant. The students from Harvard were furious. They threatened to cancel the second half of the concert. We finally persuaded them that the action had nothing to do with The College or Colonial Williamsburg, that the proper recourse was to avoid the restaurant and eat at The College or Colonial Williamsburg. Actually, the Harvard incident was one of many that sparked sit-ins, picketing and other civil rights demonstrations that finally helped bring about desegregation.

On another occasion during those difficult times, a black family registered at Colonial Williamsburg's Motor House. They asked for locker keys at the swimming pool and were issued them promptly. They became the first blacks to swim in Colonial Williamsburg. About the same time, a woman from New York called the Williamsburg Inn, said she was white and asked if her black husband would be welcome. She was asked the dates of her visit, and reservations were promptly made. In another test case, a group of white students from William and Mary accompanied black students from all-black Hampton University through the cafeteria line at the Campus Center. A cashier asked her supervisor what she should do. The answer was, "Feed them."

Against this local background, racial conflicts exploded throughout the nation. This violent situation was emblazoned on my mind one night when I was flying over Washington, D.C., en route to Norfolk. The pilot called attention to the fires burning below in the nation's capital, where rioters had turned to widespread arson. It was clear that sparks could erupt into blazes anywhere, even in Williamsburg, in those dark and dangerous days.

However, as we assessed the Williamsburg scene, we knew both races there understood the Rockefellers' position on racial matters. The family had a long record of major financial assistance to blacks, particularly for education. As far back as 1897, John D. Rockefeller, Jr., made grants to black Southern schools through the General Education Board. By 1954, this aid totaled nearly $60 million. In addition, the Rockefeller family had personally supported the black Hampton Institute at Hampton, Virginia, for twenty years before Rockefeller and Goodwin discussed the colonial restoration project for Williamsburg, located just twenty miles away.

Winthrop Rockefeller once told of a poignant incident at Hampton Institute that helped shape his personal attitude on race relations:

> To round out our education, Mother and Father believed in taking us children on trips to various parts of our country and, as we grew old enough, to foreign lands.

AN ESPECIALLY POPULAR PART OF THE "ONCE UPON A TOWN" TOUR FOR CHILDREN
IS A ROUSING STORY SESSION WITH ONE OF THE TALENTED STAFF MEMBERS.

The earliest trip I can remember—one that had a great influence on my later thinking—was a visit during the Easter vacation to Hampton Institute, a Negro normal school at Hampton, Virginia. The school program started with grade school and went on through high school, with special emphasis on agriculture and vocational trades.

The Dean of Men at the school was Major Moulton, a wonderful, elderly Negro gentleman; a man of tremendous stature physically, with a spirit as great as his body. They told a moving story about him that happened on one of his trips to New York—a story that helps to explain the very real influence he had upon the students in the school and, possibly, on me as well.

On this occasion, as he was about to cross a street he saw a little girl dart out, trip and fall in the path of a streetcar. The car couldn't possibly stop in time to avoid running over the child—but Major Moulton leaped forward, caught the girl up in his arms, and saved her life, at a very real risk to his own.

A policeman on the corner asked Major Moulton if he might have his name to report his courageous act. But Major Moulton, with the humility that was so characteristic of him, smiled and told the officer that the name wasn't important.

"Just record it as 'a Negro,'" he said.

Fortunately, someone in the passing crowd recognized him and heard his answer. The story impressed me as a boy, and in later years the memory of his simple, sincere and modest attitude helped me to a deeper understanding of the rewards we may find in relations with men and women of different race and color.

The Rockefellers also were active supporters and participants in the earliest days of the Urban League and the United Negro Fund. Another positive factor for good race relations in

Williamsburg was that blacks benefited directly from employment on restoration activities and income generated from them. Williamsburg's black community was noted for having many home owners; a large number of black high school graduates, many of whom went on to college; and an enviable standard of living compared with most other areas in the South.

As part of the volatile national scene, students at The College of William and Mary decided to demonstrate for civil rights (with a few streakers thrown in on late night forays). But their outbreak was sedate by national standards. A few students with placards asked permission to ride briefly on Colonial Williamsburg buses as part of a protest action. We had no problem with that: The students were always given exhibition building and bus passes anyway.

Students also asked the City of Williamsburg for permission to march from The College down the historic Duke of Gloucester Street to the Capitol and back. Permission was granted. The "march" looked more like a funeral procession. About a hundred students and a few professors (who parked their Mercedes out of sight) walked stoically in line, military-style. Williamsburg Police Chief Andy Rutherford escorted the group by striding with the first phalanx of the "troops." Mayor Vernon M. Geddy, Jr., watched the "demonstration" with other members of the City Council and City Manager Frank Force.

As events unfolded it seemed the City of Williamsburg, The College, Colonial Williamsburg and the community at large were likely to escape violence. Out of this threat, however, Williamsburg undertook a leadership role in Virginia and the South to bring about racial integration without explosions or blazes. The tempo of reaction was expressive without bombast.

When the racial clouds cleared, the Williamsburg community looked back on more tranquil times when positive racial attitudes had formed in the area. Mr. and Mrs. John D. Rockefeller, Jr., had laid the groundwork for harmonious relations through their many friendships with blacks. As a result, the black community appreciated the Rockefellers and their keen interest in the total welfare of Williamsburg.

This deep affection for the Rockefellers was demonstrated on March 2, 1950, when Clara Byrd Baker dedicated a plaque at Bruton Heights School in memory of Mrs. Rockefeller, who had died in 1948 and who had made the school for blacks possible. Mrs. Baker was a teacher, and her husband was the sexton at Bruton Parish Church.

"Mrs. Rockefeller recognized the dignity of simplicity, the worth of character, the power of kindness, the influence of example, the improvement of talent and the virtue of patience as paramount requisites for the fulfillment of a noble life," Mrs. Baker said. "She had courage for the great tasks of life and patience for the small ones."

Mrs. Rockefeller's son John D. Rockefeller 3rd took time to come from New York to attend the memorial to his mother, a gesture widely and warmly welcomed by the black community and their white neighbors.

Rockefeller, Jr., upon receiving a copy of Mrs. Baker's comments from John 3rd, replied, "It was, indeed, a beautiful address and would, I know, have pleased Mama greatly with the background of the large attendance of colored people, all gathered to express their continuing gratitude and sincere affection for her."

The Rockefellers' acts of generosity, friendship and understanding over the years set an example that helped improve race relations throughout the area—The College, the town and the state.

PRESIDENTIAL "SEARCH" BEGINS

News that dramatic changes in the leadership of Colonial Williamsburg were looming hit me in 1976 during a six-hour round-trip drive from Williamsburg to Lynchburg, Virginia, with Carl Humelsine. We were on a mission to investigate some antiques as possible gifts for the Governor's Mansion in Richmond, one of our many outside activities.

"Don," Humelsine said about one hour out of Williamsburg, "I've talked with the Rockefellers and the Board of Trustees about the future leadership of Colonial Williamsburg when I step down as President. Unfortunately for you, we are too much the same age, and as I see it, we have to start looking for someone in his forties who is an educator and a fund-raiser, someone with business and management experience, to run CW in the future."

Startled by the introduction of such a major subject during a casual auto trip, I readily agreed with the concept for the organization's future management.

Slowly, the enormous task of planning the change of command, the continuity of leadership, the delicacy of moving away to some extent from the Rockefeller family after fifty years of direction and financing, the complex management and policy decisions that would unfold—all began to sink in. The initial shock gradually gave way in the months ahead to excitement and anticipation. Big change at the top was in the wind, for sure! And there was the related question of how far the repercussions would spread throughout Colonial Williamsburg.

During the fifty years since Rockefeller and Goodwin first met, Colonial Williamsburg had grown into the largest privately operated preservation, restoration, interpretive and educational indoor-outdoor museum of its kind in the world. The recaptured Historic Area now embraced 173 acres of buildings, gardens and greens. A greenbelt area of 3,000 more acres protected most of the colonial part of the town once familiar to the early patriots. Thirty-six colonial crafts demonstrated in scores of exhibition buildings and other related facilities were in place representing daily life of the early Virginia colonial capital along with an outstanding and growing collection of seventeenth- to early nineteenth-century English

CHARLES R. LONGSWORTH, THE LATEST PRESIDENT OF COLONIAL WILLIAMSBURG, LOOKS
TO THE FUTURE STANDING ON THE GREEN IN FRONT OF THE GOVERNOR'S PALACE.

~ 144 ~

and American furniture and furnishings. Facilities for research, film production, book publishing, seminars and forums, plus Williamsburg's many other offerings, attracted nearly 1,000,000 Americans and our guests from more than 100 countries every year. The cost of operating the Historic Area and its educational programs now topped $22 million annually.

During the Humelsine years, the Historic Area and related projects had burgeoned. In place were a new Information Center, the Abby Aldrich Rockefeller Folk Art Center, the Motor House and Cafeteria, and the Lodge West Wing and Conference Center. Carter's Grove Plantation had been acquired, Wetherburn's Tavern had been restored, and many other historic buildings had been saved or reconstructed and opened to the public. Automobile traffic had been restricted on the Duke of Gloucester Street. Innovative changes had been inaugurated in interpreting the Historic Area. Williamsburg had become an international crossroads. But, as Humelsine reflected on the overall accomplishments of his administration, he felt the hallmark was the high quality of work in all aspects of the project.

As the stage was set to transfer the presidency, it was clear to "Williamsburg watchers" that the original Rockefeller-Goodwin dream could become a colonial-contemporary nightmare if the transition were not cradled in proper hands. Those familiar with Humelsine and his "hands-on" style of management wondered how closely he would control the transition. Would he, indeed, let go? Would he continue in a related role? Or would he move back to Washington on to a broader national or even international challenge?

What happened next was "classic Humelsine," the President at his confident best. To the surprise of on-lookers, no traditional search committee was appointed. His modus operandi for all matters relied completely on his own intuition, touching bases with Trustees and others only when required. Carl's "engines of power" were ready and running. He moved ahead single-handedly in guiding the search for a new President, and soon he picked his successor. But, to his utter dismay, it didn't work!

Humelsine's choice was William M. Dietel, an in-house choice of sorts as he was President of the Rockefeller Brothers Fund in New York City. His academic credentials were excellent—a Princeton graduate with a master's and a doctorate from Yale plus post-graduate work at London University's Institute of Historical Research. Later, Dietel had taught history at the University of Massachusetts and humanities at Amherst College. And, along the way, he had served nine years as principal of the prestigious Emma Willard School at Troy, New York. Another attraction was that as a trusted adviser to the Rockefeller family, Dietel could bring financial clout when he became President of Colonial Williamsburg.

Therefore, Humelsine launched a crafty and extended courtship of Bill and Linda Dietel. All traps were baited and carefully set. First, Humelsine invited the Dietels to visit Colonial Williamsburg. Then he introduced them to the gamut of the Williamsburg restoration, the fruition of twenty years of hard work. The Dietels "felt the rush" as the wooer extolled Williamsburg's architecture, collections, gardens, the crafts and archaeology projects, its long and proud history as the touchstone of the founding of the democratic republic through the work of George Washington, Patrick Henry, Thomas Jefferson and their helpers.

The Dietels were very impressed with the Humelsine portrayal of the Williamsburg scene but even more impressed with the President's ardent salesmanship as he plotted his succession.

"There was no search committee procedure, so we didn't realize right off what was going on!" Dietel said later. "Then Carl introduced us to Lewis Powell [Associate Justice of the U.S. Supreme Court and Chairman of Colonial Williamsburg]. We were absolutely dumbfounded!"

Finally, Humelsine popped the question to Dietel in a dressy package wrapped in embellishments so attractive he knew his target could not refuse. But, to Humelsine's complete dismay, Dietel politely declined the "once in a lifetime" offer.

"As much as I love Colonial Williamsburg and as much as I would have loved to do it, I told Carl the timing was all wrong for us," Dietel recalled.

Humelsine did not take the news in his usual good spirits. In fact, his first reaction was more akin to "How dare you say 'no'?" After surviving the first shock, however, he threw up his empty hands, regrouped and declared, "Then you've got to find someone." Dietel was taken aback at this sudden assignment, but moments later it dawned on him that he did indeed have a candidate, in fact, a great one.

"Carl," Dietel said, "I do have a guy who would be a lot better than I—you've got to meet Chuck and Polly Longsworth."

Dietel, who later became a Trustee of Colonial Williamsburg, explained that his wife and Polly Longsworth had both gone to Emma Willard and that Charles Longsworth was a magna cum laude graduate of Amherst College and a member of Phi Beta Kappa. After graduating from the Harvard Graduate School of Business Administration, Longsworth had joined the Campbell Soup Company and later had moved to the advertising firm of Ogilvy, Benson & Mather, Inc., before returning to Amherst College.

Dietel had met Longsworth at Amherst in 1960 and watched him prepare the college for its first successful fund-raising campaign. During the course of the campaign, Longsworth became interested in the concept of a new college that was being encouraged by the President of Amherst. Known as Hampshire College, the institution was first proposed in 1958 by a committee from the University of Massachusetts, Mount Holyoke, Smith and Amherst colleges. Dietel said Longsworth was the first person hired by the new college. As Vice President, he had secured the initial funding, and as Hampshire's first President, he bought the land and launched the enterprise.

The new "candidate" sounded very good to the disappointed Humelsine. Soon, escorted by the Dietels, Chuck and Polly Longsworth arrived in Williamsburg for a secret weekend overview. With a laugh, Dietel introduced the Longsworths to the Humelsines and the "search" was off again. Mary and I were invited to the welcoming dinner, and it was clear from the first cocktail that Longsworth was of presidential caliber.

During the evening, I was able to talk with Longsworth alone about the budding development program I was then shepherding.

"Colonial Williamsburg has had the world's best fund-raising program—one man, John D. Rockefeller, Jr.," I said to Longsworth. "But we know this can't last forever, and we are preparing to create an active, public fund-raising program. I know of your successful fund-raising at Amherst and Hampshire College, and we need help to find a top-notch director of development."

Longsworth's quick advice was very constructive and, through his research and interest, he helped us establish an office of financial development.

Later, as I reflected on the evening, not knowing if we even had a "bite," I realized what a tremendous job it would be for anyone to become the fourth President of Colonial Williamsburg, succeeding three very successful men. Colonel Arthur Woods, a trusted Rockefeller adviser and confidante in New York City, had been the first President and with his appointment a pattern of paternalism began. John D. Rockefeller, Jr., watched carefully over all operations from the outset in 1928. In 1935, Kenneth Chorley, also a Rockefeller lieutenant in New York, took over as President following Woods and continued the paternalistic approach of Rockefeller-supervised management until Carlisle H. Humelsine was appointed President, in 1958. Under Humelsine's administration the pattern of leadership slowly changed, particularly following Rockefeller's death in 1960. Trained by General George C. Marshall in World War II, the third President developed a strong sense of authority, replacing much of Rockefeller's decision-making with his own.

Who could measure up to the high standards set by such predecessors and cope at the same time with new and changing times? The challenge would include dealing successfully with an expanding museum-preservation field, a changing work force and governmental regulations.

While continuing to search for a suitable successor, Humelsine nevertheless slowed the process after his initial disappointment. Unlike Dietel, Longsworth was an unknown quantity to him, and thus required more investigating. The task was complicated by many other serious matters, and it was March 1976, four months after their first meeting, before Humelsine finally decided to recommend the New Englander for election as the fourth President of Colonial Williamsburg. The Longsworths had not been to the Historic Area before their meeting with Humelsine, but they found the restoration project "fascinating, enchanting." Longsworth accepted.

When all things appeared to be moving ahead and Humelsine and Longsworth had agreed to an employment package, a setback occurred. To Longsworth's surprise and discomfort, Humelsine suddenly informed him that Chairman Lewis F. Powell, Jr., had pointed out that the employment agreement had to be approved by the Board of Trustees. This procedure delayed matters, but Longsworth was elected at the next board meeting, and in 1977 he took over as President and Humelsine moved up to become Chairman, succeeding Justice Powell.

Humelsine and Longsworth subsequently occupied offices just across the hall from each other in the Goodwin Building, and soon evidence surfaced that Humelsine was planning to make the transition a slow one. For example, he retained the title of Chief Executive Officer for two years before letting go.

The interim was not always smooth. On numerous occasions I was instructed by one or the other to carry a message between their offices, separated by about four feet! One day, Humelsine referred to me as the "shuttlecock." This was an apt description. As time wore on and I was bandied back and forth, I got the feeling that I had precious few feathers left. The differences between the two highly competent men were enlarged primarily by Humelsine's presence on the scene for seven years before he retired in 1985, when he was succeeded as Chairman by Charles L. Brown of AT&T. Once, Humelsine confided to a friend, "I should never have stayed here after I stepped out as President."

One of Longsworth's conditions of employment was that he be able to continue to fly his own airplane after he became President. Both Longsworth and his wife, Polly, were accomplished pilots and had used their airplane to speed up their travels. During the earlier negotiations, Humelsine had agreed to the flying proviso, but after Longsworth was installed he told him there was some feeling on the part of Trustees that it "was not a good idea." Longsworth took his case to Richmond attorney Joseph C. Carter, Jr., Counsel and Trustee for Colonial Williamsburg. The matter was smoothed over, and Longsworth continued to fly.

Shifting the responsibilities of greeting and entertaining international dignitaries worked smoothly at first as Humelsine disavowed interest in that duty, saying it was Longsworth's job now—"I've done that." In 1984, however, Humelsine said he himself would greet His Excellency Zhao Ziyang, Premier of the People's Republic of China, and Mrs. Zhao. Longsworth stood his ground, and official relations between the President and Chairman suffered a dive.

However, as the executives reviewed their relationship they realized that the problems of transition were similar to those in any large organization, and that while they were friendly personally any differences between them were primarily in their day-to-day business relationship. As time passed, Longsworth carefully and effectively stamped his imprimatur on Colonial Williamsburg. The earlier pattern of paternalism and centralized power gave way to more delegation of authority and other managerial improvements: committee involvement, computers for record-keeping and accounting, broader employee communication, improved performance and increased income through ticket sales, merchandizing, television advertising, and hotel and restaurant sales.

Looking to the future, Longsworth began to slow expansion of the Historic Area and related construction and placed greater focus on consolidation, interpretation and refinement of present operations. He focused on missions and goals designed "to exceed visitor expectations" and to make Colonial Williamsburg "the best place to work."

Surprisingly, along the way, the idea of an expanded educational program was resurrected. Started by Humelsine and championed by Longsworth, the educational emphasis rose phoenix-like from the ashes of the Rockefellers' discord of the 1940s and early 1950s. Longsworth revealed that when he was appointed "I was told that my first responsibility was to lead the foundation into a new phase as a teaching institution." As a result, a ten-year plan known as Teaching History at Colonial Williamsburg was created.

One emphasis of the program centered on "the lives of black persons in eighteenth-century Williamsburg that demanded representation and interpretation. . . ." By 1987, Longsworth said that through a mixture of role playing and traditional interpretation "we made rapid progress" in teaching black history. He said, too, that the thoroughness and coherence of the overall education program "are unique in the history of museums."

In addition to promoting educational programs Longsworth later undertook new projects in construction and support services. His impact was especially important in carrying on and developing fund-raising from individual donor, corporation and foundation sources.

Reviewing the record, I can say that both Presidents in their combined forty-five years of leadership greatly strengthened Colonial Williamsburg's major contributions nationally and internationally in the fields of history, research, education, preservation and conservation.

EPILOGUE

Carl Humelsine telephoned me in late 1988 from his room at George Washington University Hospital in Washington, D.C. He had been sick for some time. "Don," he asked, "you remember I talked about how my funeral plans should be patterned on those done so well for Lord Botetourt's last trip down the Duke of Gloucester Street in 1770 — six horses and a black hearse, the works?" We joshed about that scene for a while, just like old times. Then he said he planned a Christmas feast in the Humelsines' new home in Williamsburg "with champagne and caviar. If I'm still in this—hospital—I'm going to have champagne and caviar, anyway."

This was a near-final example of the joie de vivre of the "boss."

Carl Humelsine died on January 26, 1989, having left Colonial Williamsburg one more of its priceless legacies. His vision, talents, dedication and personal stewardship clearly gave Williamsburg a dynamic impact on America's historical and cultural future.

D . J . G .

HEADS OF STATE AND DIGNITARIES WHO HAVE VISITED COLONIAL WILLIAMSBURG 1953–1990

1953

May	President and Mrs. Dwight D. Eisenhower
September	His Royal Highness Prince Akihito of Japan
November	Their Majesties King Paul and Queen Frederika of the Hellenes

1954

November	Her Majesty Queen Elizabeth, the Queen Mother of England

1955

November	His Royal Highness Prince Albert of Liege, the Crown Prince of Belgium

1956

March	Signora Carla Gronchi, wife of the President of Italy
May	Dag Hammarskjold, Secretary-General of the United Nations

1957

June	President Dwight D. Eisenhower
October	Her Majesty Queen Elizabeth II and Prince Philip of England
November	His Majesty King Mohammed V of Morocco

1958

June	President Theodor Heuss of the Federal Republic of Germany
October	His Royal Highness Prince Norodom Sihanouk, Prime Minister of Cambodia

1959

January	President Arturo Frondizi and Senora de Frondizi of Argentina
March	His Majesty King Hussein of Jordan
May	His Majesty King Baudouin of Belgium

1960

July	Their Majesties King Bhumibol and Queen Sirikit of Thailand

1961

March   Prime Minister and Mrs. Tage Erlander of Sweden
July   Vice President and Mrs. Chen Cheng of the Republic of China
September   President Don Manuel Prado and Senora de Prado of Peru

1962

June   Dr. Roberto F. Chiari, President of Panama
October   His Royal Highness Hasan al-Rida al-Sanusi, Crown Prince of Libya
November   President and Mrs. Ramon Villeda Morales of Honduras
December   Japanese Cabinet Members

1963

June   President Sarvepalli Radhakrishnan of India
September   Their Majesties King Zahir and Queen Homaira of Afghanistan
October   President Josip Broz Tito of Yugoslavia
            Dr. Victor Paz Estenssoro, President of Bolivia

1964

May   President Eamon de Valera of Ireland
June   Prime Minister and Mrs. Ismet Inonu of Turkey
            Prime Minister George Papandreou of Greece
            President and Mrs. Francisco J. Orlich Bolmarcich of Costa Rica
July   Prime Minister Tanku Abdul Rahman Putra al-Hah of Malaysia
October   President and Mrs. Diosdado P. Macapagal of the Philippines

1965

March   President and Mrs. Maurice Yameogo of Upper Volta
May   President and Mrs. Chung Hee Park of the Republic of Korea

1966

March   Prime Minister Indira Gandhi of India
June   His Majesty King Faisal Ibn Abd al-Aziz Al-Saud of Saudi Arabia
September   General and Mrs. Ne Win, Chairman of the Revolutionary Council of the Union of
            Burma

1967

May   Vice President and Prime Minister Yen Chia-kan of the Republic of China
September   The Japanese Cabinet
            President and Mrs. Diori Hamani of Niger
October   Prime Minister and Mrs. Terence O'Neill of Northern Ireland
            President and Mrs. Lyndon B. Johnson
            Prime Minister and Mrs. Lee Kuan Yew of Singapore
            Their Majesties King Mahendra Bir Bikran Shah Deva and Queen Ratna Rajya
            Lakshmi Devi Shah of Nepal
November   Crown Prince Vong Savang and Princess Manilay Vong Savang of Laos
            President and Mrs. Lyndon B. Johnson

1968

March	President and Mrs. Alfredo Stroessner of Paraguay
April	His Majesty Olav V, King of Norway
May	President Habib Bourguiba of Tunisia
June	President Jose Joaquin Trejos Fernandez of Costa Rica

1969

April	His Majesty King Hussein of Jordan
May	Prime Minister and Mrs. John G. Gorton of Australia
	Prime Minister Petrus J. S. de Jong of the Netherlands
June	President and Mrs. Carlos Lleras Restrepo of Colombia
October	His Imperial Majesty Mohammad Reza Pahlavi, The Shahanshah of Iran, and Her Imperial Majesty Farah Diba Pahlavi, The Empress of Iran

1970

April	Prime Minister and Mrs. Hilmar Baunsgaard of Denmark
May	President and Mrs. Soeharto of Indonesia
July	Dr. Urho Kekkonen, President of Finland
October	President and Mrs. Nicolae Ceausescu of Romania
November	Vice President and Mrs. Nguyen Cao Ky of South Vietnam

1971

March	President and Mrs. Richard M. Nixon
April	President and Mrs. Franko Malfatti of the Commission of the European Community
	President Richard M. Nixon and Vice President Spiro T. Agnew
May	His Majesty King Faisal of Saudi Arabia
September	The Japanese Cabinet

1973

April	Prime Minister and Mrs. Giulio Andreotti of Italy
	Her Majesty Queen Rambhai Barni of Thailand
July	Ambassador Han Hsu of the People's Republic of China
	His Imperial Majesty Mohammad Reza Pahlavi, The Shahanshah of Iran, and Her Imperial Majesty Farah Diba Pahlavi, The Empress of Iran
September	Prime Minister Ali Bhutto and Begum Bhutto of Pakistan
October	Ambassador Haung Chen of the People's Republic of China

1974

September	President and Mrs. Giovanni Leone of Italy
October	Prime Minister and Mrs. Gough Whitlam of Australia
	His Excellency Edward Gierek, Polish First Secretary and Mrs. Stanislawa Gierkowa
	His Royal Highness the Duke of Gloucester, Richard Alexander Walter George
November	Dr. Bruno Kreisky, Chancellor of Austria

1975

March	Prime Minister and Mrs. Dzemal Bijedic of Yugoslavia

April	Prime Minister and Mrs. Hedi Nouira of Tunisia
May	His Imperial Majesty Mohammad Reza Pahlavi, The Shahanshah of Iran, and Her Imperial Majesty Farah Diba Pahlavi, The Empress of Iran
June	President and Mrs. Walter Scheel of the Federal Republic of Germany
September	President and Mrs. Alfonso Lopez of Colombia
	Their Majesties Emperor Hirohito and Empress Nagako of Japan
October	President and Mrs. Anwar Al-Sadat of Egypt
December	Prime Minister Gaston Thorn of Luxembourg

1976

January	President and Mrs. Gerald R. Ford
March	Prime Minister and Mrs. Liam T. Cosgrave of Ireland
April	His Majesty Carl XVI Gustaf, King of Sweden
	The Right Honourable Jules Leger, Governor General of Canada, and Madam Leger
May	The Earl of Dunmore, John Alexander Murray
June	Delegation of Parliamentarians of the United Kingdom
July	Chancellor and Mrs. Helmut Schmidt of the Federal Republic of Germany
August	Dr. Urho Kekkonen, President of Finland
September	President William R. Tolbert, Jr., of Liberia
October	President and Mrs. Gerald R. Ford and Governor and Mrs. Jimmy Carter
November	Vice President and Mrs. Nelson A. Rockefeller
	Vice President Nelson A. Rockefeller and Secretary of State Henry Kissinger
December	His Royal Highness Prince Gyanendra and Her Royal Highness Princess Komal of Nepal

1977

February	President Jose Lopez Portillo of Mexico
June	President Carlos Andres Perez of Venezuela
November	His Imperial Majesty Mohammad Reza Pahlavi, The Shahanshah of Iran, and Her Imperial Majesty Farah Diba Pahlavi, The Empress of Iran

1978

April	His Imperial Highness Prince Hitachi and Her Imperial Highness Princess Hitachi of Japan
May	President Kenneth David Kaunda of Zambia
November	Her Royal Highness Crown Princess Sonja of Norway

1979

April	His Excellency S. Sonoda, Minister of Foreign Affairs of Japan
September	Dame Te Atairangikaahu, Queen of the Maori
November	Prime Minister and Mrs. Jack Lynch of Ireland

1980

June	His Excellency Qian Xinzhong, Minister of Public Health, People's Republic of China
November	His Excellency Dr. Lansana Beavogui, Prime Minister of Guinea

1981

April	His Royal Highness Prince Charles, Prince of Wales
	Mr. and Mrs. Richard M. Nixon

August	The Right Honourable Lord Mayor of London, Colonel Sir Ronald Laurence Gardner-Thorpe and the Lady Mayoress
October	President and Mrs. Ronald W. Reagan
	President and Mrs. François Mitterand of France
	Vice President and Mrs. George Bush

1982

April	Her Majesty Queen Beatrix and His Royal Highness Prince Claus of the Netherlands

1983

May	President and Mrs. Ronald W. Reagan
	President François Mitterand of France
	Prime Minister Pierre Elliott Trudeau of Canada
	Federal Chancellor Helmut Kohl of the Federal Republic of Germany
	Prime Minister Yasuhiro Nakasone of Japan
	Prime Minister Amintore Fanfani of the Republic of Italy

1984

January	His Excellency Zhao Ziyang, Premier of the People's Republic of China, and Mrs. Zhao
June	His Excellency Junius Jayewardene, President of Sri Lanka, and Mrs. Jayewardene
November	Their Royal Highnesses, the Grand Duke and Grand Duchess of Luxembourg

1985

April	President Belisaro Betancur of Colombia and Mrs. Betancur
	Ambassador Hernan Felipe Errazuriz of Chile
	Mrs. Yasuhiro Nakasone of Japan
May	President Ronald W. Reagan
October	Ambassador and Mrs. Emmanuel de Margarie of France
	His Imperial Highness, Prince Naruhito of Japan

1986

August	Ambassador and Mrs. Nobuo Matsunaga of Japan

1987

July	Ambassador and Mrs. Yuri Dubinin of the Union of Soviet Socialist Republics
August	Ambassador and Mrs. Tommy Koh of Singapore
November	Ambassador and Mrs. Antony Acland of the United Kingdom

1988

April	The Honorable Sir Antony Acland, Ambassador from the United Kingdom, and Lady Acland
July	Marshall Sergei Akhromeyev, Chief of the General Staff of the Soviet Armed Forces

1989

February	Her Royal Highness Princess Margriet of the Netherlands
June	Vice President Daniel Quayle

August	President Henriquez Delvalle of Panama and Mrs. Delvalle
September	His Majesty Carl XVI Gustaf, King of Sweden
October	His Royal Highness Philippe of Belgium
	Ambassador Emmanuel de Margarie of France
	President Roh Tae Woo of the Republic of Korea and Mrs. Roh
November	Prime Minister Kamisese Mara of Fiji

1990

March	Ambassador and Mrs. Kjell Eliassen of Norway
April	Ambassador and Mrs. W. Susanta De Alwis of Sri Lanka
May	The Honorable Sir Antony Acland, Ambassador from the United Kingdom, and Lady Acland
	Ambassador and Mrs. Bensid of Algeria
	Ambassador Edmund Hawkins Lake of Antigua and Barbuda
	Ambassador and Mrs. Sebele of Botswana
	Ambassador and Mrs. Datin Siti Suhanah Binti Pham of the State of Brunei Darussalam
	Ambassador and Mrs. Velichkov of Bulgaria
	Ambassador Kavakure of the Republic of Burundi
	Ambassador Pondi of Cameroon
	Ambassador and Mrs. Mosquere of Colombia
	Ambassador and Mrs. Issombo of the Congo
	Ambassador and Mrs. Sallah of The Gambia
	Ambassador and Mrs. Herder of the German Democratic Republic
	Ambassador and Mrs. Hussain of India
	Ambassador and Mrs. Al-Mashat of the Republic of Iraq
	Ambassador and Mrs. MacKernan of Ireland
	Ambassador and Mrs. Johnson of Jamaica
	Ambassador and Mrs. Afande of Kenya
	Ambassador and Mrs. Van Tonder of the Kingdom of Lesotho
	Ambassador Eugenia A. Wordsworth-Stevenson of the Republic of Liberia
	Ambassador and Mrs. Rajaonarivelo of Madagascar
	Ambassador and Mrs. Mbaya of Malawi
	Ambassador and Mrs. Toure of Mali
	Ambassador and Mrs. Stellini of Malta
	Ambassador U Myo Aung of Myanmar
	Ambassador and Mrs. Sainju of Nepal
	Ambassador Zulfigar Ali Khan of Pakistan
	Ambassador and Mrs. Al-Badrawi of the State of Qatar
	Ambassador and Mrs. Mamba of the Kingdom of Swaziland
	Ambassador Charles Musana Nyirabu of Tanzania
	Ambassador and Mrs. Vejjajiva of Thailand
	Ambassador and Mrs. Wendt of Western Samoa
	Ambassador and Mrs. Chigwedere of Zimbabwe
	The Permanent Representative of Bolivia to the Organization of American States and Mrs. Rolon Anaya
June	Vice President Daniel Quayle
August	Ambassador Johan Meesman of the Netherlands
September	Prime Minister D. B. Wijetunge of Sri Lanka
	Mrs. Suzanne Mubarak, wife of President Mubarak of Egypt

INDEX

Page numbers in italics refer to photographs.

Abbott, Stanley, 30
Abby Aldrich Rockefeller Folk
  Art Center, 43, 45
  stenciled wall gallery, *48*
Allen-Byrd House, *111*
Annenberg, Mr. and Mrs.
  Walter, 71–72
Antiques Forum, 74, 75

Baker, Clara Byrd, 143
Bassett Hall, *32*
  bedroom, *47*
  bought by Rockefellers, 43
  decorated by Abby Aldrich
    Rockefeller, 43
  dining room, *46*
  entrance hall, *42*
  front façade, *41*
  history and description, 40, 43
  neighbors, 45–49
  parlor, *45*
Bhumibol, King of Thailand,
  114–115
Black, Shirley Temple, 107,
  108, 109
Blagojevich, Elizabeth, 71
Blagojevich, Miodrag, 71
Blue Bell Tavern, *125*
Boothe, Armistead, 131–133
Brinkley, David, 73, 75, 127
Bruton Parish Church, *24*, 27,
  50
  interior, *81*
  wedding of Winthrop Paul
    Rockefeller and Deborah
    Cluett Sage, 57, 59

Busch, August, Jr., 56–57
Bush, George, *107*

Carter, James Earl, Jr., *106*
Carter's Grove Plantation
  acquisition, 52, 55
  description, 55
  façade, *54*
  legends about, 55–56
  slave dwelling preservation,
    59
  Winthrop Rockefeller's gifts
    to, 56
Ceausescu, Nikolae, *115*,
  115–116
Champion, Marge and Gower,
  119
Charles, Prince, *120*
Chorley, Jean Traverse, 89, 91,
  119
Chorley, Kenneth, 25, 148
  card game with Churchill,
    88–89
  with Eisenhower and
    Churchill, *90*
  initial meeting with, 22
Churchill, Sir Winston
  with Eisenhower, *85, 89, 90*
  Williamsburg visit, 87–89,
    91
College of William and Mary
  civil rights demonstration,
    143
  dedication of Phi Beta
    Kappa Memorial Hall, 29
  students asked to dine with
    Rockefellers, 49
  Wren Building open to
    public, 56

Commonwealth of Virginia
  bestows honorary citizenship
    on John D. Rockefeller,
    Jr., 124
  liquor-by-the-drink issue,
    127
  relations with Williamsburg,
    124–128

Darden, Colgate, 127–128
DeWitt Wallace Fund for
  Colonial Williamsburg, 71
DeWitt Wallace Gallery for
  the Decorative Arts, 71,
  73
Dietel, William M., 146–147
Disney, Walt, 109–110

Economic Summit leaders at
  Williamsburg, *122*
Eisenhower, Dwight David
  with Churchill, *85, 89, 90*
  talk with Gonzales, 84,
    86–87
  Williamsburg visit, 84,
    87–88, 89, 91
Elizabeth, Queen Mother of
  England, *118*, 119
Elizabeth II, Queen of
  England, 116–117, *118*
Employees-to-Williamsburg
  project, 70
Endowment fund, 70
Enrichment Fund, 64
Ernst, Joseph W., 16

Faisal, King of Saudi Arabia,
  113–114
Faubus, Orville, 23

Ford, Edsel, 28
Ford, Gerald, *105*
Fosdick, Raymond B., 43
    observations about Rocke-
        feller, 30
Fund-raising development
    program, 68–75

Gandhi, Indira, *120*
Garrett, Wendell, 75
Godwin, Mills E., Jr., 78, 127,
    128
Gonzales, Donald J., *135*
Goodwin, Rev. W. A. R.
    with John D. Rockefeller, *24*
    letter to Edsel Ford, 28
    search for benefactor for
        Williamsburg restoration,
        25–30
Great Oak at Bassett Hall, *42*
Gridiron Club dinner in
    Williamsburg, 77–83

Hennage, Joseph, 72
Hennage, June, 72
Hirohito, Emperor of Japan,
    111–113, *112*
Holton, Linwood, 137
Humelsine, Carlisle H., *135*
    accomplishments of his
        administration, 146, 148
    citizens' committee to
        furnish the Governor's
        Mansion, 137
    diplomatic visitor entertain-
        ment, 102
    elected President of Colonial
        Williamsburg, 18, 25
    fund-raising development
        program, 68–75
    head of Virginia commis-
        sions and boards, 128
    King of Morocco's visit,
        110–111
    letter to Armistead Boothe,
        133
    letter to Gonzales, 134, 136
    search for successor,
        146–149
    and sermon by Rev. Lewis,
        82
    U.S. Bicentennial Commis-
        sion chairman, 129

with Winthrop Rockefeller,
    53
Hussein I, King of Jordan, 113,
    121

James Geddy House, 56
Johnson, Lady Bird, 76
Johnson, Lyndon Baines, 76
    Bruton Parish Church
        services, 79, 82
    visit to Williamsburg,
        77–83

Kekkonen, Urho, 109
Kingsmill Plantation
    acquisition, 52, 55
    Anheuser-Busch purchase of,
        56–57
Kohl, Helmut, *122*
Kyger, R. W., 36, 37

Lewis, Rev. Cotesworth
    Pinckney, sermon during
        Johnson's visit, 79, 80, 82,
        83
Longsworth, Charles R., 68,
    130, 145
    fund-raising letter to Armis-
        tead Boothe, 131–133
    selection by Humelsine as
        successor, 147–149

Martin, Dave, 99, 101
Martin and Woltz advertising
    agency, 96, 99
Martin's Hundred, 56
McCrea, Mary C. "Molly,"
    55
McHenry, Barney, 73
McKenzie Apothecary, 56
Michener, James
    Library of Congress project,
        95
    Williamsburg visit, 93–95
Mohammed V, King of
    Morocco, 110–111
Morecock sisters, 45–49
Morris, Mrs. George M., *74*

Nagako, Empress of Japan,
    111–113
Nakasone, Yasuhiro, *123*
Nixon, Richard Milhous, *105*
Noël Hume, Ivor, 56

Official visitors list, 151–156
"Once Upon a Town" tour, 97,
    142
O'Neill, Abby, 31, 72
O'Neill, George, 31, 72
Osborn, Fairfield, 26, 28
Ox cart with children, *98*

Pahlavi, Mohammad Rezi, *121*
Peyton Randolph House, 56,
    100
Philip, Prince, 116–117
Pinckney, Rev. Cotesworth, 76
Pleasants, Alec, *139*
Pulaski Club, 36–37

Race relations
    College of William and
        Mary civil rights demon-
        stration, 143
    desegregation of Colonial
        Williamsburg facilities,
        140–141
    Hampton University student
        march, 140–141
    Harvard Glee Club visit,
        141
    test cases, 141
Radock, Mike, 68
Raleigh Tavern Society, 73, *74*,
    75
Reader's Digest employees-to-
    Williamsburg project, 70
Reagan, Ronald, *106*
Restoration accomplishments
    over fifty years, 144, 146
Rockefeller, Abby Aldrich, 35,
    38, 65
Rockefeller, David, 113
Rockefeller, David, Jr., 141
Rockefeller, John D., *62*
    children, *58*
Rockefeller, John D., Jr., 32,
    58, 148
    with Abby Aldrich Rocke-
        feller, *35*, 65
    with Alec Pleasants, *139*
    attraction of Williamsburg,
        39
    community relations, 33–34,
        36–37, 39
    conservation projects, 26
    death and memorial service,
        66–67

dedication of Phi Beta
Kappa Memorial Hall at
College of William and
Mary, 29
differences with John 3rd
over Williamsburg's
mission, 51–52
Enrichment Fund, 64
family's support of restorations after his death, 68
history of relationship with
Rev. Goodwin, 26–30
with Humelsine and
Chorley, 23
initial meeting between
Gonzales and, 25
interest in restoration
project, 21
local church attendance, 37,
39
personal benefaction total,
68
personal role in restorations,
34, 36, 37
plans for Williamsburg, 29
post–World War II restoration ideas, 63–64
Pulaski Club membership,
36–37
with Rev. Goodwin, 24
secrecy of involvement, 33
unconditional gift to
Williamsburg, 66
Rockefeller, John D. 3rd
card game with Churchill,
88–89
differences with his father
over Williamsburg's
mission, 51–52
interest in restoration
project, 21
Rockefeller, Laurance, 73
Rockefeller, Nelson, 61, 66
visits to Williamsburg,
44–45
Rockefeller, Winthrop
with Abby O'Neill, 31
Arkansas prison riot, 23
at Arkansas ranch, 19
army career, 20–21
Carter's Grove gifts, 56,
59
Carter's Grove Plantation
acquisition, 52, 55

Chairman of the Board of
Trustees of Colonial
Williamsburg, 52
decision to run for Governor
of Arkansas, 22–23
early visit to Williamsburg
anecdote, 28–29
Gridiron Club dinner
speech, 77, 78
gubernatorial campaigns, 52
Hampton Institute incident,
141–142
idea for book about
Williamsburg restoration,
16
initial meeting with, 18–21
insight about family affection for Williamsburg,
30–31
King and Queen of Thailand
visit to Williamsburg, 114
memorial service, 59–60
with President and Mrs.
Carlisle H. Humelsine, 53
at son's wedding, 59
Rockefeller, Winthrop Paul
with Deborah Cluett Sage,
50
wedding, 57, 59
Rockefeller Brothers Fund, 72
Rockwell, Norman, and
Williamsburg ad
campaign, 99, 101
Roosevelt, Eleanor, 104
Roosevelt, Franklin Delano,
102, 103
Rusk, Dean, 116, 117

Sage, Deborah Cluett, 50
wedding, 57, 59
Sirikit, Queen of Thailand,
114–115
Sleepy Hollow Restorations,
17
Stillinger, Elizabeth, 75

Teaching History at Colonial
Williamsburg, 149
Thaler, F. Roger, and fund-
raising development
program, 68, 70, 71
Truman, Harry S., 104

Virginia. See Commonwealth
of Virginia
Virginia Commission of the
Arts and Humanities, 128

Wallace, DeWitt
Colonial Public Hospital
support, 71
DeWitt Wallace Fund for
Colonial Williamsburg, 71
DeWitt Wallace Gallery for
the Decorative Arts, 71,
73
employees-to-Williamsburg
project, 70
with Lila, 69
Michener's visit to Williams-
burg, 93
support for restorations, 71,
72–73
Wallace, Lila, with DeWitt, 69
Wetherburn's Tavern, 56
Whitlam, Gough, 123
Winchester, Alice, 74, 75
Winthrop Rockefeller Charita-
ble Trust, 72
Woods, Col. Arthur, 29, 148

Zaharov, John, 37
Zhao Ziyang, 149

ABOUT THE AUTHOR

A native Nebraskan, Donald J. Gonzales is a graduate of the University of Nebraska and was a Nieman fellow at Harvard University. Before his twenty-five years at The Colonial Williamsburg Foundation, he spent sixteen years as a United Press correspondent covering the White House and State Department. He won the National Headliner Award "for outstanding achievement in domestic news reporting."

Gonzales spent most of his career with Colonial Williamsburg as Vice President for Public Affairs, where his journalism background was put to good use on press relations, special events, advertising, travel development and program planning. His expert press bureau and public relations department became models for museums and foundations throughout the country. As Senior Vice President, he also served as chief administrative officer in the President's absence. Mr. Gonzales served on the board of directors for the Public Relations Society of America, is a former chairman of PRSA's international committee and is past president of the Old Dominion Chapter.

After retiring from the Foundation he started his own firm consulting on executive management, fund-raising, public relations and tourist promotion with organizations throughout the United States. He continues to write for Colonial Williamsburg publications and has been published in many national magazines. He is the author of *Travel and the Arts*.

An avid pilot, he enjoys flying "because there are no committees and no telephones." He was trained to fly twelve kinds of fighter planes during World War II and has since flown more than thirty kinds of planes. Active in many public service projects in Virginia, Gonzales is also a trustee of the Interlochen Center for the Arts. He and his wife, Mary, a professional organist/pianist, have four children and six grandchildren, and divide their time between Williamsburg, Michigan and Mexico.